Michelle Cottam is a Londoner, historian, and author. Her first book, *Maybe It's Because I'm a Londoner*, was published in 2020. Michelle has had a keen interest in the history of London since childhood when a trip to the Tower of London inspired her lifetime passion for history. Her writing style is intriguing and captures the attention of a wide range of audiences. Michelle Cottam's analysis of history and facts makes this book a compelling read and she has the ability to fascinate even the less experienced reader.

In loving memory of Ella.

Michelle Cottam

CHARLES DICKENS: A PEOPLE'S PERSON

AUSTIN MACAULEY PUBLISHERS™

LONDON • CAMBRIDGE • NEW YORK • SHARJAH

A CIP catalogue record for this title is available from the British Library.

ISBN 9781528974240 (Paperback)
ISBN 9781528974257 (ePub e-book)

www.austinmacauley.com

First Published 2023
Austin Macauley Publishers Ltd®
1 Canada Square
Canary Wharf
London
E14 5AA

Thank you to my friends who joined me on my Charles Dickens guided walk in 2018. You were so interested in what I had to say about Dickens that it inspired me to further my knowledge and write this book.

A huge thanks to David for his patience, continual support, and reassurance that this book was worthwhile submitting to my publisher.

Alex, it was after your enthusiastic visit to the Charles Dickens Museum, which until then I never knew existed, that prompted my first visit to Dickens' former family home.

Table of Contents

Preface

In this book, I have written some fictional scenes from some of the poignant recollections that Charles Dickens experienced as a child.

Chatham Kent, Around 1821

A little boy's cheeks are glowing red, almost the same colour as his kite – as he runs as fast as he can, trying to catch his breath, clutching his kite tightly as it blows recklessly against the strong sea wind. He takes a glimpse in front of him of the picturesque boats in the naval harbour in Chatham Kent. He keeps on running. These are the happiest days of his life and he never wants them to end. "Charleeey," someone bellows out his name in the distance behind him. It is a familiar voice, it is his mother, Elizabeth Dickens. "Charles, it's time to get ready for school," she shouts louder as her soft voice gets drowned in the wind. He turns around and starts running towards her until he catches up and stops as she reaches out and lifts him up off the ground. He giggles as she embraces him affectionately. She smiles at him as she lowers him back onto his feet and takes his hand and holds it tightly as they walk together and head back home. She walks with pride and looks so young and carefree, not a worry in the world as she waves to the locals and the passing sailors. She could never imagine at that moment the devastating affects her husband's, John Dickens, debts would have on their peaceful lives and how quickly this happiness would soon come to a sorrowful

abrupt end, causing her happy little boy Charles so much
sadness and pain.

Foreword:
The Journey of Writing
This Book

If you are wondering how I came about writing this book about Dickens, then let me explain. I knew that it was going to be a big challenge but it happened by chance. I had taken a group of friends on a Charles Dickens guided walk a few days before Christmas in 2018. As I started my research, I headed down to my local library to gather my very first books on Dickens. I would rummage through the books and was so delighted when I found loads of books by Dickens. I began to read as many books as I could find on Dickens, searching in and out the shops for books until I had my own collection. My books varied from those written by well-known authors, some by less well-known authors, children's books and educational books. I wanted to get different perspectives about Dickens. I began to get really interested as I read the books and was surprised how much I enjoyed learning not just about the life of Dickens but also about life in nineteenth century, London. So here my new book begins…

Chapter 1
The First Global Celebrity?

Charles Dickens, the most popular novelist of the century and one of the greatest humourists that England has produced. These are the words of John Forster taken from his biography, *A life of Charles Dickens, Chapter 1, Earliest Years 1812–1822.* John Forster's biography was published in 1872–1874. He was a trusted and lifelong friend of Charles Dickens who would seek advice from him on the novels that he was writing. Did you know that Charles Dickens has been described as the first global literacy celebrity? Charles Dickens certainly enjoyed the limelight, loved entertaining and was a bit of a showman! Despite his fame, he was loyal to his readers and worked hard to give them one hundred percent. He gave the public plenty of opportunities to meet him as he went on hundreds of public tours where he would read and act out scenes from his books, especially the dramatic parts from characters like the violent, criminal Bill Sikes in *Oliver Twist*. The atmosphere in the room would be electric as Charles Dickens would bring the characters of his books alive just by reading his books as he acted their characters out so realistically. It was as though they were real people in the room. His audience would clap with emotions, shiver with excitement and get goosebumps. They would laugh, cry and even sometimes faint! He had a gift of being able to engage with his audience and was friendly and entertaining, meeting him was an experience his fans and audience enjoyed so much that they never forgot it. He was a young man in the 1830s, during the romantic movement when fashion was dramatic and flamboyant with huge sleeves and hats. King William IV was on the throne between 1830 and 1837. When Charles Dickens published his first novel in 1837, *The Pickwick Papers,* Queen Victoria was on the throne. Charles Dickens enjoyed life as an adult, he enjoyed parties, playing games, taking a stroll down to the market, smoking cigars, good food, wine and company. He had a large circle of friends that were articulate, such as novelists, actors, actresses, publishers, artists, playwrights and his good friend the heiress Angela Burdett Coutts with whom he helped establish a house to reform the poor 'fallen women' in society. This was typical of Charles Dickens always wanting to help people and despite his success as an author and his comfortable life, at the back of his mind was always the poor. He was also concerned about the welfare of people that society had appeared to have forgotten like those in prisons and asylums. Although we cannot meet Charles Dickens today, he will never be forgotten. He is still one of the most popular authors and has one of the most recognised faces of any author. His books continue to be as popular as ever and have never been out of print. Charles Dickens and John Forster had a very close friendship. Charles Dickens trusted him and wrote to him frequently seeking advice on many topics, such as Forster's opinion on the manuscripts he was writing and about his personal life. Forster was also close to the Dickens family, he was a God parent to Charles Dickens' daughter, Mary. Charles Dickens was one of London's most famous residents! Not just famous in London, we must never forget that Dickens travelled widely in Europe and North America as a famous global writer! He was also respected by many authors such as his friend George Eliot and royalty, such as Queen Victoria, who enjoyed reading *The Pickwick Papers* and *Oliver Twist*. Everyone had an opinion on his books including the poet and playwright, Oscar Wilde. When Charles Dickens died, Queen Victoria sent her condolences. Charles Dickens had more passion for London than anyone I have ever heard of. He lived in London for most of his life and nearly all his books have references to London. His knowledge of London was extraordinary not unlike The London Encyclopaedia which is packed with information on the history of the streets and places in London. Charles Dickens created some of the world's best-known characters that people still love and find familiar today. They socialised in real places like the inns and landmarks in London. Many of these places still exist today, even Charles Dickens childhood home in Ordinance Terrace, and so does his family home, which he shared his wife Catherine in Doughty Street. Tell me someone that you know that has not heard of the reformed miser Ebenezer Scrooge from Charles Dickens' most successful book, *A Christmas Carol*. His books are loved and enjoyed so much that even in Charles Dickens' day, when the poor people couldn't read or write, they would still pay a halfpenny for the cheaper edition so that someone could read their copy to them.

Chapter 2
Never Judge a Book by Its Cover

Dickens got so much satisfaction from writing his books but as he became more successful, his schedule to produce them soon became very demanding. He wrote books right up until the end of his days. His writing was a full-time job that gave him an income. He worked very hard, often late at night, so that he could meet his deadlines. He was interested in reading from a young age. Some of his favourite books are still just as popular today, such as, *Robinson Crusoe and Arabian Nights*. His father, John Dickens, had a large collection of books in their home in Chatham which Dickens would read for hours. Dickens' style of writing was popular because he wrote about the social issues of the poor and his books appealed to all types of people. He could relate to a poor working-class family because of his father's debts. Those debts often meant that his family had no spare money and left him with painful memories and feelings of being ashamed when he was young. He recalled feeling devastated as his parents sold the family furniture and other sentimental items like the large collection of books that he treasured and loved to read. This went on for month after month until the house was finally bare. John Dickens' problems with debt continued to haunt Charles in his adult life. When Dickens was making money as a successful author, he often had to pay off his father's debts. The characters in his books were very real to him as they were based on real people, such as friends and family. The stories he wrote about were based on fact. *A Christmas Carol* was inspired by a visit to Field Lane Ragged School where he witnessed many scenes of distress. Dickens himself only had a few years formal education. Many authors of his time were middle class like the Bronte's. Dickens came from a border line middle class family. When he wrote *Dombey and Son* in 1848, he was in competition with many accomplished authors. For example, classic books were being published by respected authors, such as Charlotte Bronte who wrote *Jayne Eyre* in 1847 and Emily Bronte who wrote *Wuthering Heights* also in 1847. William Makepeace Thackeray, who knew Dickens, wrote *Vanity Fair* and published it in a monthly serialised between 1847 and 1848, it was hugely popular. Despite all this competition, Dickens' books became popular. In the 1830s and 1840s, Charles Dickens became the most famous author of his time.

Chapter 3
Getting to Understand Dickens

It has been a slow but exciting process of understanding Dickens' character. Realistically how can you really know what someone was like when you have never met them! Reading books, biographies and memoirs written by Dickens' family, friends and acquaintances may give a good account of his personality and character. We think we know someone but often we do not. There are two sides to every story so for that reason I have avoided writing in detail about certain things that I feel that I am not able to make a judgement on. Biographies about Dickens contain detailed accounts by people who knew him well and from stories by his children which reveal personal and intimate stories of their relationship with their father. Dickens' early biographers would have been able to speak to him directly or to people who knew him. Dickens' books alone can speak for themselves, they are written with compassion, pity, humour and wit which requires intelligence by someone who is aware of the human emotions. He seemed to be a bit of an eccentric and had a pet raven called Grip! *The Life of Charles Dickens* was written by John Forster between 1872 and 74. It is a biography of Dickens, partly in Dickens' own words, and the information comes from Forster's private collection of letters from Dickens. Some of the letters include Dickens' painful recollections from his childhood when he worked at Warrens Blacking factory at only 12 years old. Dickens' father, John Dickens, was sent to the Marshalsea prison, which was a debtor's prison. Dickens had to leave school and work in the factory to pay for food and help pay off his father's debts. When Dickens told his story about these memories, it was a shock to his friend Forster who had no idea because Dickens had kept it secret for years and up to then had not even told his family.

Chapter 4
Dickens' Wonderful
World of the Theatre

Times have changed an awful lot since Dickens' days, especially with modern technology. We live in a time when everything can be done quickly, like writing which can be typed quickly. Dickens spent hours every day writing his books by hand using a quill pen and paper. In his early days, there would not have been any gas lighting and he would have only had dim candlelight so he would have strained his eyes. Dickens also experienced major changes in his lifetime, especially during the beginning and late Victorian times. London expanded and the population soared with the new development of the railway which replaced the traditional horse-drawn coaches. People could now travel quite easily in and out of London from the countryside on a day trip. *Sketches by Boz* are short stories written by Dickens between 1833 and 1836 and describe everyday life giving us a detailed account of life in the nineteenth century. People and their opinions have changed so much over the centuries; however, you can often still see Victorian traits in modern people that have been passed down from their ancestors. I often see someone in the street that reminds me of a character straight out of a Dickens book! It is something about them, for example, it could be their body language so when you watch them pass you as they stroll down the street, you can imagine that they resemble characters out of Dickens book. It could be a Sam Weller, a Mr Pickwick or even a Mrs Gamp, they are all still out there! Dickens thought very carefully when he chose the names of his characters they often resembled, cockney working-class Londoners. We all occasionally get a nostalgic feeling that bring us back to a memory in the past. The other day when I was typing away writing this book and concentrating deeply in my thoughts, I noticed a chiming in the background. It was my old-fashioned mantel clock in my living room chiming away on the hour. As I listened to the familiar melody, I imagined that Dickens also listened to the chimes of his clocks in his study as he wrote his novels. Clocks chiming to mark the hour were an important part of life in Dickens' days. By listening to the number of chimes striking from a nearby church may have been the only accurate way that some people could know the time. Church bells were important to Dickens and they are referred to many times in his books. In *A Christmas Carol*, the spirits of Christmas visit Scrooge in his bedroom and he is awoken by the loud chime of his clock and is aware of the time by counting the chimes ringing out. When the first of the three spirits visit Scrooge, the Ghost of Christmas Past, the clock chimes loudly at one o'clock in the morning with a deep dull hollow melancholy ONE. One thing that was clear to me when I first began researching and writing about Dickens was how important London, and Londoners, were to him and that they played a huge part in his books. From a young age,

Dickens had a sense of humour and enjoyed mimicking and entertaining people. He would entertain his family with his sister by singing their favourite songs to them. He loved the theatre and it probably all started when the stepson of his mother's sister, James Lament, who lived with the Dickens family in Bayham Street took him to the theatre when he was very young. He was kind to Charles and made him a toy theatre which he also painted for him. There was also the serious compassionate side of Dickens that I soon discovered when I began reading some of his most popular books such as *Oliver Twist* and *David Copperfield*. These books highlight his awareness of misfortune and the hardship of life living in poverty in London, especially for the poor families and children. Dickens' observation and attention to detail of different types of people is said to have made him a good mimic and it often represents someone that is emotionally intelligent. In his books, he gives his characters names that he has chosen carefully that are often witty and entertaining. The Victorian nurse, Mrs Gamp, in the book *Martin Chuzzlewit*, is said to represent a stereotype of a nurse in the early Victorian era. A type of an umbrella was called a gamp and Mrs Gamp always carried one. Charles Dickens would often base his characters on real people and he would alter their names, so they were similar. Some of his most popular characters were Mr Pickwick, Mr Micawber, Miss Havisham, Bob Fagin and the artful Dodger. Bob Fagin was the real name of a boy he met when he worked in the Blacking factory. Dickens' books also quite importantly give the message that being wealthy does not necessarily bring you happiness and it can change or ruin people by making them have hard feelings and becoming unkind.

Chapter 5
Dickens' First Attempt
of Writing a Novel

Dickens wrote numerous books in his lifetime and began writing in his early 20s. By the time Dickens was 30 years old, he was a very successful and famous author and had already written *The Pickwick Papers*, which was the beginning of his success as well as *Nicholas Nickleby, Oliver Twist* and *The Old Curiosity Shop*. Dickens' first published work, *A Dinner at Poplar Walk*, appeared in the London periodical, *The Monthly Magazine* in 1833. It was Dickens' first attempt of writing fiction at the age of 21 as an unknown author and he was not paid for it. The story goes that he dropped the manuscript off late one night in *The Monthly Magazine's* post box. He was not paid for the story and his name as the author was not included. It did not matter to Dickens because he was over the moon to see it in print!

Stealthily one evening at twilight, with much fear and trembling, into a dark letter-box in a dark office up a dark court in Fleet Street, he discovered that it had been published only when he went back to buy the next issue of the magazine.

It was then he saw that his story, *A Dinner at Poplar Walk,* was in the next issue of the magazine! "I walked down to Westminster Hall and turned into it for half-an-hour because my eyes were so dimmed with joy and pride that they could not bear the street and were not fit to be seen there." Over the next few months, Dickens wrote another eight stories for *The Monthly Magazine*! It was later included in *Sketches by Boz* with the new title, *Mr Minns and His Cousins*, and he went on to write six more stories over the next year. So how did Dickens' career as a journalist begin? After leaving school at the Wellington House Academy in 1827, he worked for Ellis and Blackmore as a junior clerk between 1827 and 1828. He was a likeable young man and made everyone laugh with his gifted mimicry and his impersonations of his colleagues, the lawyers and clerks and the clients. He began to go to the theatre every day and became a member of the Garrick Club. In those days, the club was in Drury Lane in one of the rooms of the Theatre Royal. The story goes that he landed an audition at the Theatre Royal where the manager George Bartley and actor Charles Kemble were to see him. Dickens prepared for the audition every day for long hours but the audition did not eventually take place because he had to miss it because he was unwell with a bad cold. He was devasted and many people would agree that he may have been an actor instead of a writer if he had been able to go to the audition. There is no doubt that he was a good actor and was influenced by William Shakespeare. Dickens wrote books all his life but he was also an amateur actor while he was writing his books and he would oversee the whole theatre production, the cast, lighting, props etc and write and even act in his plays. His Christmas stories and adaptions from his books would be played at the Lyceum Theatre which Dickens knew very well and the Adelphi Theatre in the Strand. Dickens was also inspired by the character acting of Charles Matthews who was famous at the Adelphi Theatre. Dickens' public readings later in life were so lifting and inspiring because of his love for performing at the theatre.

In 1827 to 1828, Dickens worked in the law offices of Ellis and Blackmore as a junior clerk. He taught himself shorthand while renting a room at Furnival's Inn. Dickens left Ellis and Blackmore to become a freelance reporter at the Doctors Commons between 1829 and 1831. By 1831, Dickens was working as a parliamentary reporter. In 1833, *A Dinner at Poplar Walk* was published by *The Monthly Magazine*.

Chapter 6
Sketches by Boz

In 1834, Dickens became a reporter on the Morning Chronicle and worked for George Hogarth, his future father-in-law. It was after several visits to George's family home in Fulham that Dickens got friendly with his daughter Catherine. It was Dickens' career as a journalist that gave him the experience to write for a living and earn an income from it. George Hogarth gave him a job which was an opportunity that would change his life for ever. He would be paid for his published stories which were a collection of stories he had written called *Sketches of London* under the name of Boz while he was working for George Hogarth. In 1835, the *Morning Chronicles* launched an evening edition called the *Evening Chronicles* in which Charles Dickens was asked by George Hogarth to write *Street Sketches*. In 1836, the publisher John Macrone approached Dickens with the idea of collecting the Sketches together into a volume and reprinting them under the name *Sketches by Boz*. During this time Dickens was living at Furnival's Inn, Holborn. Macrone offered Dickens one hundred pounds for the copyright of the book with the illustrations by the popular illustrator George Cruikshank. The famous George Cruikshank was very well-known as a caricaturist and illustrator of books. To have Cruikshank's name on *Sketches by Boz* was a huge steppingstone and guaranteed Dickens would become known as an author with the publicity and promotion of the book. Dickens added new pieces like *A Visit to Newgate*, which is one of his most compelling accounts of a prisoner in the notorious prison. Dickens' stories were published in a monthly series until they were eventually made into books. *Sketches by Boz* is a collection of observations of London. Dickens became well known because of the success of *Sketches by Boz*. Boz was Dickens' pen name in his early years as an author and was a family nickname. *Sketches by Boz* was published every month between 1833 and 1836 and sold for a shilling until it was eventually published in a single volume in 1839. Dickens married Catherine Hogarth in 1836 while his career was beginning to take off. Many of Dickens' books started as monthly serials that were then collated into a single edition. Every month readers would look forward to the next issue. His readers found it exciting that the story unfolded each month. Each monthly issue which would become a chapter in the single edition. This style of writing produced many cliff-hangers as each monthly issue was designed to keep the reader interested and convince them to buy the next month's issue. Dickens was able to see the response from his audience by doing this and sometimes would slightly change the plot and characters based on their response. However, it was hard work meeting the deadlines each month as sometimes he would be working until late at night on two novels at the same time. Dickens' first novel, *The Pickwick Papers*, was published monthly between 1836 and 1837. After Dickens' success of *Sketches by Boz*, his publishers, Chapman and Hall, approached him to write *The Pickwick Papers*. Dickens was asked to write descriptions for a series of comic pictures for a Cockney Sporting club. The first cartoon plates were by the illustrator Robert Seymour who was the first illustrator of *The Pickwick Papers* until his tragic death in April 1836. Dickens then hired the illustrator Robert William Buss to illustrate the third instalment. Dickens replaced him with Hablot Knight Browne known by his pen name Phiz to illustrate the subsequent instalments. *The Pickwick Papers* was originally called *The Posthumous Papers of the Pickwick Club*. It is a story about a group of friends and the main characters are Samuel Pickwick, the founder of the Pickwick Club, Sam Weller and Alfred Jingle. The stories became popular when the cockney character Sam Weller was introduced after the first few episodes. One of the most popular stories in *The Pickwick Papers* is about a trial at the Guildhall London of Mr Pickwick and Mrs Bardell for a breach of promise. In *The Pickwick Papers*, Mr Pickwick and Sam stayed at the George and Vulture when they were in London. The George and Vulture still exists today and is a restaurant in Castle Court near Lombard Street in the City of London. Dickens was a frequent visitor at the George and Vulture. *The Pickwick Papers* was published in 19 issues over 20 months but Dickens missed one of the deadlines for *The Pickwick Papers*. There was no issue in May 1837 because on May 7, 1837, Mary Hogarth, Catherine Dickens' 17-year-old sister, tragically died at their home in Doughty Street London. Dickens like his wife Catherine was overwhelmed with grief and shock by her sudden death and was too upset to write so the May issue was not produced.

Chapter 7
Charles Dickens' London

Most of the places Dickens wrote about in his books are places where he had visited and were known to him like the Taverns and the Guildhall in London which housed the Court of Common Council until 1873. London's Guildhall is home to the Corporation of London today. Dickens made hundreds of places that he visited famous by writing about them in his books. He also highlighted the awful conditions for the poor children in the workhouses, schools and the slums of London. In Dickens' early books, London was essential for generating material to write about. He needed to walk through the busy noisy London streets every day to be inspired and to feed his imagination for the book he was working on. Many of Dickens' books such as *Oliver Twist* focus on the dangers of being an orphan and living in poverty in London. In *Oliver Twist*, Dickens focuses on the slum districts like Clerkenwell and Saffron Hill. The last section of Saffron Hill was called Field Lane, this was the location for Fagin's den in Oliver Twist. Hatton Garden which runs off Saffron Hill was once an area of squalor, poverty, and crime. Number 54 Hatton Gardens is where Dickens sets the police office and magistrates court run by Mr Fang in *Oliver Twist* and it is where Oliver is brought after being arrested for picking Brownlow's pocket. It has been said that this area was behind the inspiration that led Dickens to write *A Christmas Carol* in 1843, after Dickens visited the Field Lane Ragged School for the poor children in September 1843 and he was devastated by what he witnessed. Dickens wrote about the slums, otherwise known as the rookeries, in areas of London such as St Giles rookery near Oxford Street and at the Bleeding Heart in Holborn. The slums are long gone today but St Giles church and the Bleeding Heart Tavern still exist today. When new streets and railways were built in the late 1800s, the slums slowly began to be cleared away. Dickens also mentioned in his books other parts of London that were not slums such as Mayfair Square, Grosvenor Square and Cavendish Square. These were places that were being occupied by the wealthy. Today these areas in London are still known to be occupied by wealthy landlords. Cavendish Square appears in many street settings in Dickens' books. The dishonest banker Mr Merdle in *Little Dorrit*, who commits suicide when finally bankrupted, resided in Harley Street. In *Nicholas Nickleby*, Madame Mantalini the dressmaker also has her premises there. Dickens makes a point in his books that the wealthy characters are miserable. Many places Charles Dickens wrote about still exist today and cause a huge amount of interest from visitors not just in the United Kingdom but also from around the world. Dickens enthusiasts visit London and other parts of the country, such as the Dickens former family house in Doughty Street London and Gad's Hill Place in Higham, Kent, where Dickens spent his final days.

Chapter 8
Travelling Abroad

Dickens also wrote about the places that he visited when on tour in Italy, France, Switzerland and America. He lived in Lausanne for a year where he began writing *Dombey and Son*. When Dickens travelled on his public reading tours to Britain, Ireland and America, he would take his portable writing desk with him. He took this iconic desk with him which he had designed himself. It was designed so that it was waist high and had a slightly raised platform so that he could place the elbow of one arm on the platform and turn the pages of his book using the other arm. The reading desk also had a lower shelf to place a carafe of water on. Dickens would spend hours standing up as he read out to his audience. The reading tours were dramatic and entertaining with a sound board placed behind Dickens and gas lamps giving out a dramatic lighting effect. The experience was like watching a performance at the theatre.

Chapter 9
Bibliography

After the success of *The Pickwick Papers*, Dickens was approached by the publisher Richard Bentley, who asked him to be the first editor of the magazine *Bentley's Miscellany* in 1836. It was a position Dickens held until 1838. After *The Pickwick Papers*, he began his first instalments of *Oliver Twist*.

Oliver Twist was first titled the *Parish Boy's Progress* in *Bentley's Miscellany* where it was published in monthly instalments between 1837 and 1839 again with the illustrator George Cruikshank. It was adapted into a three-volume book in 1838 under the new title *Oliver Twist*. *Oliver Twist* is one of the most popular stories and was one of Dickens' favourites it gives an insight of the reality of being poor in early Victorian London. The story is about an orphan called Oliver who is born in a workhouse and after being treated cruelly runs away to London where he meets the Artful Dodger who is a member of a gang of child pickpockets led by an elderly criminal called Fagin. The story highlights child labour, the cruel treatment of orphans in London and the harsh treatment of pupils by headmasters in schools.

Nicholas Nickleby was Dickens' third novel and had as the original title *The Life and Adventures of Nicholas Nickleby*. It was again published by Chapman and Hall. Dickens began writing *Nicholas Nickleby* while he was still working on *Oliver Twist*. Around this time Dickens' books were being adapted into performances at the theatre. Charles Dickens would often take part in the acting. *Nicholas Nickleby* was also first published as a serialised book between March 1838 and October 1839, then it was published in a book format. The illustrator this time was Hablot Knight known as Phiz. *Nicholas Nickleby*, who is the main character, is a story about the life and adventures of Nicholas Nickleby, a young man who must support his mother and sister after his father dies.

The Old Curiosity Shop was one of two novels which followed next, the other being *Barnaby Rudge*. These books were published as short stories in Charles Dickens' weekly serial *Master Humphrey's Clock* between 1840 and 1841 and were printed in book format in 1841 by Chapman and Hall. *The Old Curiosity Shop* is about a young girl called Nell, who is an orphan and lives with her grandfather in the Old Curiosity Shop in London. Like many of the places Dickens wrote about the Old Curiosity Shop still exist today in Holborn, London and dates to the sixteenth century. When Dickens wrote his book, it was an antique shop but after he had written the book it was given the same name as the book's title *The Old Curiosity Shop*.

Dickens first historical novel *Barnaby Rudge* (1841) is based on the real-life events of the Gordon Riots of 1780. The Gordon Riots were several days of rioting in London led by anti-Catholic Lord George Gordon. It was published by

Chapman and Hall and was serialised from February to November in 1841.

A Christmas Carol was first published on the December 19, 1843 by Chapman & Hall and the illustrator was John Leech. 6,000 copies were printed in the first edition and were sold out by Christmas Eve.

The Life and Adventures of Martin Chuzzlewit, later known just as *Martin Chuzzlewit,* was originally serialised each month between 1842 and 1844. In 1844, it was published as a book by Chapman and Hall. This book was known for being one of the least popular of Dickens' books but Dickens regarded it as one of his best works. The illustrations are by Phiz. When Dickens went on his first American tour in 1842, he kept a travel log called *American Notes*. These were the inspiration for writing *Martin Chuzzlewit. Martin Chuzzlewit* is set mainly in America and Martin is the main character of the selfish Chuzzlewit family. In the book, Dickens was accused of being critical of the Americans and their civilisation. He dedicated the novel to Angela Burdett-Coutts, 1st Baroness Burdett-Coutts (1814–1906) who was a good friend of Dickens. Angela Burdett-Coutts was known in her time as the richest heiress in Victorian England and was the first woman to be presented with the Freedom of the City of London in 1872. Like Dickens, Angela Burdett-Coutts is also buried at Westminster Abbey.

Dombey and Son also appeared as a monthly serial between October 1846 and April 1848. It was published as a novel in 1848 by Bradbury & Evans and illustrated by Phiz. The original title of the book was *Dealings with the Firm of Dombey and Son*: *Wholesale, Retail and for Exportation.* Dickens began writing *Dombey and Sons* in Lausanne,

Switzerland and completed it in Paris and England. Dickens often wrote when he was touring or on holiday whether it was abroad or at the English seaside. In *Dombey and Sons*, Dickens writes about social indifference for the poor. *Dombey and Son* is about Paul Dombey, who is a wealthy owner of a shipping company, who dreams of having a son to continue his shipping business. When his son is born, his wife tragically dies shortly after giving birth, Dombey is bitter and neglects his eldest child who is a girl.

David Copperfield is the eighth novel by Dickens and was first a serial called, *The Personal History Adventures, Experience and Observation of David Copperfield, the Younger of Blunderstone Rookery*. It was first published in serial format between 1849 and 1850 and as a book in 1850. It was published by Bradbury & Evans and illustrated by Phiz. The novel is about the main character David Copperfield, giving an account of his many struggles and hardships when his widowed mother marries again. The book resembles many events in Dickens own life as a young boy. *David Copperfield* is said to be the book which is most likely to be an autobiography of Charles Dickens. *David Copperfield* was Dickens' favourite novel. It seems that he based it on events in his own life, and described it as, "A very complicated weaving of truth and invention." David's fascination with beautiful Dora Spenlow can be compared with Dickens' feelings for the real-life Maria, who was his first love. In *David Copperfield*, David, at ten years old, is sent to London to work in the wine warehouse where his job was to paste labels on the wine bottles. When Dickens was ten years old, his father was sent to the debtor's gaol, so Dickens had to leave school and was sent to work in Warrens Blacking

Factory where his job was to paste the labels on pots of boot blacking. When the Dickens family joined their father in prison, Charles Dickens had to lodge with Elizabeth Rylance a friend of his mother. In David Copperfield, David lodged at the home of the Micawber family. Mr Micawber was wonderful with words, just like Dickens' father, but was also always in debt. Mr Micawber and his family also ended up in a debtor's prison. The Micawber's are said to be based on Charles Dickens' own parents. Dickens, as a young political journalist, learnt how to write shorthand and David Copperfield also learns how to write shorthand and writes books to earn a living.

Bleak House was the next novel and first published in a series between March 1852 and September 1853. It was also published by Bradbury and Evans and illustrated by Phiz. It was published in book format in 1853. The novel is told mainly by the novel's heroine, Esther Summerson and partly by a narrator. This appears to be an unusual style of writing for Dickens. Esther Summerson tells her own story using the past tense. As a child she is raised by her godmother Miss Barbary but unknown to her, her real mother is Lady Dedlock. Esther's father was Captain Hawdon who was Lady Dedlock's lover before she married Sir Leicester Dedlock. Lady Dedlock believes that Esther is dead. There is a house named Bleak House in Broadstairs but this is not the original Bleak House in the novel. Dickens stayed with his family at that house which was then called Fort House for at least one month every summer between 1839 and 1851. Fort House was renamed Bleak House in Charles Dickens' honour after his death. Dickens locates the fictional Bleak House in his book at St Albans, Hertfordshire.

Hard Times, formally known as *Hard Times: For These Times*, is the tenth novel by Dickens. It was first published in weekly parts between April 1854 and August 1854 in a weekly magazine called *Household Words*, edited by Dickens and as a book in April 1854. It was published by Bradbury & Evans. It is unusual compared to Dickens' other novels as it does not have any illustrations or a preface, and it is also the only novel written by Dickens that does not have any scenes set in London. The novel is set in a fictitious Victorian industrial town called Coketown. Coketown is a typical northern English mill-town. The story describes English social and economic conditions in areas such as Manchester and Preston. Although Coketown is a fictional town in England, Dickens highlights the conditions of some of the factories in those towns. The main character in the novel is Superintendent Mr Gradgrind who runs a school in Coketown.

A Child's History of England is a history book and appeared in serial form in *Household Words* between 1851 and 1853. These stories were published in a book format between 1852 and 1854. They were published in three volumes by Bradbury & Evans. Charles Dickens dedicated this book to his children, "My own dear children, whom I hope it may help, by and by, to read with interest larger and better books on the same subject." Dickens novels are based on real facts and real-life experiences.

His next novel, *Little Dorrit,* is another story based on Dickens' experiences. The story he shares with the reader has many similarities to Dickens' own childhood. Originally published in serial form between 1855 and 1857 the illustrations are again by Phiz; it was published in a book form by Bradbury and Evans in 1857. The story revolves around the main character, Amy Dorrit, who is the youngest child of her family, she has two older siblings. Amy Dorrit was born and raised in the Marshalsea prison. Her mother died when she was eight years old and she financially supports herself and her father by making money in the prison by sewing. She is devoted to her father, William Dorrit, who has been in the Marshalsea prison for over 20 years. He is embarrassed to be in the debtor's prison, so Amy keeps her sewing to support her father a secret outside the prison. The novel highlights and criticizes the prison system and the Marshalsea debtors' prison where the prisoners were unable to leave until they had paid off their debts. In those days, the whole family would also have to live in the prison. Dickens understood what he was writing about when he wrote about the Marshalsea debtor's prison. His own father, John Dickens, was imprisoned there with his family. In the novel, he uses the setting of the prison to give a real-life account of life in prison both for the prisoners and their families. Like Dora, Dickens kept his father's time in prison a secret until years later when he told his friend John Forster. Dickens went to work in Warren's Blacking factory when he was just a young boy to earn money and support his family. He had to give up his schooling and the impact of the dramatic change in circumstances had an emotional impact on him for the rest of his life. Dickens who would have supper in the prison in the evenings with his family and visit for the day on Sunday with his elder sister Frances, known as Fanny. In the novel, *Little Dorrit*, Amy Dorrit also has a sister called Fanny. The character Little Dorrit is said to be based on a real-life character, Mary Anne Cooper, who was a family friend.

Chapter 10
Charles Dickens, the Historical Novelist

Dickens had a talent for writing historical novels. *A Tale of Two Cities* is said to be his best-known work of historical fiction and his bestselling novel. The other historical novel he wrote was *Barnaby Rudge*. *A Tale of Two Cities* is set in London and Paris before and during the French Revolution. Dickens had a keen interest in history and it has been said that he had read *The French Revolution: A History by Thomas Carlyle* which was published in 1837. It has been described as one of the best pieces Dickens ever wrote. It was first published in a weekly serial between April and November 1859 and then published as a novel in 1859. The book is illustrated by Phiz and published by Chapman and Hall. The main characters are a French Doctor, Dr Alexandre Manette, who has been in prison for 18 years and his daughter Lucie Manette. Lucie is loved by two men, an English lawyer and a French aristocrat, who look like twins but are not. Lucie being in love with the Frenchman marries him, but he is sentenced to die at the guillotine as an enemy of the Revolution.

The French Revolution began on the May 5, 1789 and ended on November 9, 1799. It began when the common people overthrew the monarchy and established a republic. King Louis XVI's government was blamed for mishandling a financial crisis in the 1780s. King Louis XVI was the last king of France and was executed for treason by guillotine.

The famous opening sentence in *A Tale of Two Cities* describes the destruction of the French revolution very dramatically. "It was the best of times, it was the worst of times, it was the age of wisdom, it was the age of foolishness, it was the epoch of belief, it was the epoch of incredulity, it was the season of Light, it was the season of Darkness, it was the spring of hope, it was the winter of despair, we had everything before us, we had nothing before us, we were all going direct to Heaven, we were all going direct the other way-in short, the period was so far like the present period, that some of its noisiest authorities insisted on its being received, for good or for evil, in the superlative degree of comparison only."

Chapter 11
Dickens Mania

Great Expectations followed *A Tale of Two Cities* and was Dickens' 13th novel. Dickens was a known author at this stage and was travelling widely on reading tours. He was so famous now that wherever he went, he was recognised in the street. *Great Expectations* was first published as a series in Dickens' weekly periodical, *All the Year Round*, from the December 1, 1860 to August 1861. In October 1861, Chapman and Hall published the novel in three volumes. The novel is set in Kent and London and is about an orphan called Pip. Pip meets an escaped convict, and he takes pity on him. This novel has been described as a classic with the character of Miss Havisham, a wealthy spinster who is a recluse after being jilted at the altar on her wedding day and still sits around waiting in her old decaying wedding dress. Pip falls in love with her adopted daughter, Estella, but Estella is only beautiful on the outside and is hostile towards Pip. She does not know how to be affectionate because Miss Havisham has brought her up not to love anyone.

Our Mutual Friend followed next and was the 14th and the last completed novel that Dickens ever wrote. It was serialised between 1864 and 1865 by Chapman and Hall and published in book format in 1865. The cover of the original book is by Marcus Stone, the son of Frank Stone, the illustrator and a friend of Dickens. The story is set in London and highlights the greed and corruption that money can bring. The main character is John Harmon who is the heir to the Harmon estate on the condition that he marries, Bella Wilfer, a beautiful girl born into poverty.

The Signal-Man is a first-person ghost story by Dickens. It was first published as part of the Mugby Junction collection in the 1866 Christmas Edition of *All the Year Round*.

The Mystery of Edwin Drood was the final novel by Dickens but was not completed. It was originally published in April 1870 and illustrated by Samuel Luke Fildes. The novel was scheduled to be published in 12 instalments between April 1870 and February 1871. However, only 6 were ever completed. The book is set in Cloisterham which could resemble Rochester. The novel is focussed on Edwin's uncle, John Jasper, who is a murder suspect when Edwin Drood mysteriously goes missing. When Dickens died unexpectedly on June 9, 1870, the novel was left unfinished, only 6 of a planned 12 instalments had been published. Dickens left no plans for the remaining instalments, but there have been many adaptions and continuations by writers who have attempted to finish the story. *Charles Dickens* revealed the murder mystery conclusion of the novel to those close to him. The novel is named after a character, Edwin Drood, who disappeared and is supposedly murdered. Although his suspected killer is not revealed, suspicions point towards his uncle John Jasper.

Chapter 12
Catherine the Brave

Although this book concentrates on Dickens, the author, I think it is important to show how significant his wife, Catherine Dickens, was. She was a big part of his life for a long time and it seems that she only wanted to be loved by her husband. She had 10 children, which was not unusual in those days, and accompanied Dickens on his overseas tours to Europe and on his first tour to America when they were away from home for at least 4 months.

These journeys were often in harsh conditions and without the modern transport that we have today. The journeys would have been exhausting and hard work for a young mother who had to leave her children behind. Catherine supported her husband until their separation in 1858. Her younger sister Georgina, who Dickens considered to be a close friend, never married or had children, would often accompany them on holidays in England and help look after the children. She would eventually step into Catherine's shoes at parenting them and look after the children full time. When Catherine separated from Dickens and moved out of the family home, Georgina stayed and looked after the children also running the household. It was a role that she fulfilled until Dickens' death.

In Dickens' days, travelling abroad could be exhausting and time consuming, especially traveling by sea or on land travelling in a coach on steep and bumpy roads in Europe. Traveling by sea, especially in the winter, would have been cold and wet and a nightmare journey especially if you suffered from sea sickness. A trip to North America in those days meant that you could be traveling by sea for at least seven days. It was Dickens' tours of America with his public reading in places like New York and Boston that really made him famous. When Dickens died, news of his death quickly travelled around America and Europe and people mourned him from all around the world. On January 3, 1842, Dickens, just before his 30th birthday, set off on his first voyage to America with his wife Catherine and her maid. They boarded the RMS Britannia at Liverpool and arrived in Boston, Massachusetts on January 22, 1842. As soon as Dickens arrived in America he was mobbed by fans. He enjoyed the attention at first, however, in a letter to his friend, John Forster, his frustration and despair is clear as he writes, "I can do nothing that I want to do, go nowhere where I want to go, and see nothing that I want to see. If I turn into the street, I am followed by a multitude."

Chapter 13
Bon Voyage

Dickens travelled around America and Canada by steamboat, rail and coach. He visited prisons and mental institutions which he wrote about in his journal detailing his trip to North America. Dickens enjoyed his stay at Boston where he wrote in his journal, "The air was so clear, the houses were so bright and gay. The city is a beautiful one and cannot fail, I should imagine, to impress all strangers very favourably." After Boston, Dickens also travelled to New York. Dickens was a celebrated writer of his times and still is today. He could communicate with all types of people from different backgrounds and had a vast knowledge of London because he had lived in London nearly all his life. Dickens would write about his experiences in America in his travelogue detailing his trip to North America from January to June 1842. The travelogue was published as *American Notes for General Circulation* in October 1842. *The Life and Adventures of Martin Chuzzlewit* was serialised between 1842 and 1844 and published by Chapman and Hall in 1844. The story takes place in England and America. The book is based on the title's character, Martin Chuzzlewit, who is sent to America. The book came across to some Americans as being critical of the American society.

Chapter 14
A Christmas Carol

My favourite book as a child was *A Christmas Carol,* which was known by many people simply as '*Scrooge*' for short. Even today if you only refer to the book with the name '*Scrooge*', everyone knows it is the miser Ebenezer Scrooge, and which book you are talking about! I have watched *Scrooge* dozens of times on TV especially at Christmas time when I was a child. Once I remember getting really excited as the film was about to start and shouting out at the top of my voice "*SCROOGE* IS ON" to my siblings who were somewhere else in our house! Christmas really felt like Christmas when I would watch the film.

It has never been out of print since first publication. When Dickens wrote *A Christmas Carol*, it was the beginning of the Victorian era and Christmas customs such as singing carols and decorating the home were becoming popular. Having a Christmas tree became fashionable and a tradition during the reign of Queen Victoria when Prince Albert brought a tree into Windsor Castle and decorated it with lights and sweets. Dickens, in his books, shares his memories of early Victorian London and the growing awareness of child poverty. Dickens wrote five short Christmas stories, *A Christmas Carol* in

1843, *The Chimes* in 1844, *The Cricket and the Hearth* in 1845, *The Battle of Life* in 1846 and *The Haunted Man* in 1848 but *A Christmas Carol* was always said to be his favourite. *A Christmas Carol* was an overnight success. When Dickens wrote it, the old traditions of Christmas were changing and being replaced with new ones. In the Victorian times, some people believed that Christmas was a religious festival and it should not be celebrated in a joyful way. *A Christmas Carol* soon changed many people's views and it made Christmas more popular. During the same year that *A Christmas Carol* was published the first commercially produced Christmas cards were sent and, like Dickens' Christmas book, over a hundred years later are still popular. The look of *A Christmas Carol* was very important to Charles Dickens but colour illustrations were very costly. The book was bound in red cloth with gilt-edged pages containing colourful illustrations by John Leech. In the trial edition of the book, the title page was in green and red, but the green faded rapidly so the official first edition that came out on December 19, 1843 had a title page in red and blue. The illustrations in *A Christmas Carol* are the earliest examples of hand-tinted etchings in a book. At the time of publication, one critic said, "It was a national benefit to every man and women who reads it." Although the sales were a huge success, the profits were not as much as Dickens was expecting because the production of the book was so expensive. The following year in 1844 Dickens was able to enjoy seeing *A Christmas Carol* adapted into a theatre production at the famous Adelphi Theatre in London. It is interesting that *A Christmas Carol* is written in 'staves' instead of chapters. A stave usually refers to the five lines on which musical notes are written. When *A Christmas*

Carol was first published, novels would often be read aloud in public and be a special event when families gathered. *A Christmas Carol* was a big hit and was performed almost from the moment it was first published in 1843. Dickens regularly read it aloud at public events. A passage from the novel remained part of Dickens' popular public reading right up to his death. The novel has undergone numerous adaptions for the stage, television, cinema, and the radio. When Dickens wrote *A Christmas Carol,* life was miserable for many. The cities were filthy and poverty was widespread, on top of all that the winters were freezing. *A Christmas Carol* brought a ray of sunshine and comfort into the hearts of thousands. People would listen in awe as he acted out the character of Ebenezer Scrooge and the ghost Marley. Christmas was Dickens' favourite time of year and before he wrote about the joys of Christmas in *A Christmas Carol*, he had already written other Christmas stories. *The Pickwick Papers* is one of the best examples of a good 'knees up' and having the best time of your life with the Wardle family Christmas Eve party. *The Pickwick Papers*, like *A Christmas Carol*, was a best seller. You could say that Dickens brought the magic to Christmas for many people and his Christmas books were at the top of the bestselling charts in the Christmas publishing market from the 1840s. After the success of *A Christmas Carol*, Dickens went on to write four more Christmas books, *The Chimes* in 1844, *The Cricket and the Hearth* in 1845, *The Battle of Life* in 1846 and *The Haunted Man* in 1848. *The Haunted Man* was Dickens' last Christmas book. Later in Dickens' career his enthusiasm and endless readings at Christmas eventually began to tire him. "I am sick of the thing," he confessed to a friend in 1868. In the 1830s and

1840s, Dickens became the most famous writer of his time but this brought an enormous demand for him to be available to the public. Dickens is often referred to as a Victorian writer although he lived through more than the Victorian era. The Victorian period was from 1837 until 1901, Queen Victoria's reign. When Dickens was born in 1812, George III was king of Great Britain. *A Christmas Carol* was first published in 1843, which was the beginning of the Victorian era and was very different to the late Victorian times. *A Christmas Carol* was written using references and ideas that were from the early Victorian times. When Dickens wrote *A Christmas Carol*, he was very concerned about social reform. The novel suggests that society has a responsibility to look after the poor and disadvantaged and that wealthy people and businessmen have an important role to play in society. Christmas time brought a glimmer of hope and happiness to the poor who could escape from the misery of their lives for a short time. Several famous people popularised Christmas in Britain. Dickens did this by writing *A Christmas Carol* and Prince Albert introduced the Christmas tree to Britain. However, Christmas had been celebrated in Christian Europe long before the Victorian era. Dickens is also remembered as a great social reformer. *A Christmas Carol* contains some of his attitudes on social reform. In 1842, a year before he wrote *A Christmas Carol*, he had voiced his concerns regarding child labour. Dickens' books like *Oliver Twist* raised public awareness of how poor children who were ill-treated. Dickens campaigned for children's' rights, education and social reform. Dickens was influenced by his surroundings in London when he wrote and had his own style of writing. He wrote about real people and real experiences in his life when he wrote about prisons, workhouses and poverty. When Dickens was born in 1812, there were many talented writers that were already making their mark. There were lots of classic literature writers around when he was a child such as Jane Austen, who wrote *Pride and Prejudice* in 1813 and Mary Shelley who wrote *Frankenstein* in 1818. Later in his life writers such as Charlotte Bronte, who wrote *Jane Eyre* in 1847, Emily Bronte, who wrote *Wuthering Heights* in the same year, Charles Kingsley who wrote *The Water Babies* in 1863, and in 1868 Louisa May Alcott wrote *Little Women*. Hans Christian Andersen wrote now famous fairy tales for children such as *The Ugly Duckling* in 1843 and *The Little Match Girl* in 1845. Hans Christian Andersen was a friend of Dickens and came to stay with him and his family at Gads Hill Place. George Eliot was another friend of Dickens and visited him at his home at Tavistock House, London. George Eliot was a pen name. The author's real name was Mary Ann Evans. Dickens admired her books, especially her novel *Adam Bede*, and often dined with her and her partner George Henry Lewes. The young Queen Victoria is known to have enjoyed reading Dickens' books such as *Oliver Twist*.

Chapter 15
The Social Reformer

Dickens had been aware of the diversity in London since he was a little boy and he expressed and highlighted this in his writing. Most people struggled to survive in society and Dickens transformed these people into characters in his stories. Dickens was a social reformer and used his books to highlight the issues that were important to him. By writing about social issues, he was able to bring awareness to everyone especially to the people in authority who were able to do something about it. Dickens often wrote about the effects that poverty and misfortune can have on people's lives, for example, Oliver Twist is an honest orphan raised in a workhouse who runs away to London and meets a dishonest villain, Fagin and then joins a gang of pick pockets. There is no doubt about the importance of London to Dickens. In 1846, Dickens wrote to his life-long friend John Forster (and later his biographer) about the difficulties he was experiencing with writing his latest book, *Dombey and Son*, when he was in Lausanne, Switzerland. He wrote, "A day in London sets me up and starts me," but outside the city, "the toil and labour of writing, day after day, without that magic lantern, is IMMENSE!!" It's not surprising that all his novels include a reference to London because it was an important part of his life. He came to London when he was 12 years old so was a Londoner for most of his life. Dickens also wrote about his early years as a young child in Rochester and Kent and makes it clear that these were his happiest childhood memories. However, a few years after writing to Forster about how he needed his magic lantern, Dickens seems to tire of London. In a letter to his friend, Edward Bulwer-Lytton, in February 1851 he seems to have had a change of heart as he describes London as a vile place.

London is a vile place, I sincerely believe. I have never taken kindly to it since I lived abroad. Whenever I come back from the country, now, and see the great heavy canopy lowering over the housetops, I wonder what on earth I do there, except on obligation.

Clearly Dickens enjoyed travelling abroad with his family when he promoted his books. By the end of his life, Dickens was well-travelled and had spent time in America and Italy. He enjoyed the fresh air, green scenery and the laid-back lifestyle on the continent. In those days, a trip to America would mean that if you travelled from Liverpool, you would spend at least eight days at sea. For the first time in his life, Dickens would have experienced the simpler lifestyles of people who lived in rural areas in France and Italy, where he lived for a year and compared the clean air and green landscape to the overpopulated foggy filthy London. It would have certainly been an eye opener for him. Dickens makes it obvious how much the fog in London bothered him and makes a reference about the fog being a nuisance in his book Bleak House.

Fog everywhere. Fog up the river where it flows among green airs and meadows; fog down the river, where it rolls defiled among the tiers of shipping and the waterside pollutions of a great (and dirty) city... Chance people on the bridges peeping over the parapets into the nether sky of fog, with fog all round them, as if they were up in a balloon and hanging in the misty clouds.

Dickens was able to live a private and peaceful life abroad where he was not easily recognised whereas in London people recognised his famous face all the time and were coming up to him because they wanted to speak to him and shake his hand.

Chapter 16
Take a Walk Down
Memory Lane

Some places in London Dickens wrote about have now disappeared due to redevelopment and the construction of new buildings and roads causing them to be demolished. In some parts of London, you can still retrace his characters' footsteps around London. Today in the twenty-first-century the famous landmarks he wrote about like St Paul's Cathedral and The Monument are still tourist attractions. Mansion House is still the residence of the Lord Mayor of London and The Old Bailey is still the Central Criminal Court. It is possible to visit lots of little quaint places tucked away which were the haunts of Dickens such as the Ye Olde Cheshire Cheese pub and the Bleeding Heart, which are mentioned in his book *Little Dorrit*. Lombard Street is where Dickens met his first love Maria. Places that are worthwhile visiting are Cheapside, Monument, The Old Bailey, St Paul's Cathedral, St Bartholomew's Hospital, the Bank of England, Wood Street, Poultry, Smithfield, Cornhill and, of course, the Guildhall where the famous Pickwickian trial took place. In *The Pickwick Papers*, it was at the George and Vulture that

Mr Pickwick stayed before his trial. It's worth visiting the George and Vulture just to get a sense of how London looked in Dickens' day. You may be surprised to see that it hasn't changed much. The George and Vulture is tucked away in St Michael's Alley which is a great place to stand and experience how London once looked with its narrow alleyways. Dickens visited many churches in London but St Paul's Cathedral features frequently as a setting in his stories and it is often a meeting place for his characters or where his characters listen to the bells chiming on the hour. In *Master Humphrey's Clock*, Dickens describes Master Humphrey going up to the top of St Paul's Cathedral. St Paul's Cathedral was built by Sir Christopher Wren in 1675 and was the tallest building in London for over a hundred years. The panoramic city views available today from St Paul's Cathedral were just as exciting in Dickens lifetime when he wrote,

Draw but a little circle above the clustering housetops and you shall have within its space everything with its opposite extreme and contradiction, close by.

St Paul's even then was a tourist attraction as it is today. It cost around two pence to enter the cathedral, sixpence to go to the Whispering Gallery and a shilling to see the crypt and vaults. David Copperfield takes Peggotty to the top of the dome when showing her the tourist attractions of London. When I first started writing about Dickens, I imagined him spending most of his time sitting at home in London busy writing away at his desk in his study. I did not think he had much spare time to be outdoors. Although he did spend long hours at his desk writing, he loved being outdoors and went out every day after lunch on his daily walks for a few hours during which he would walk for miles. In his early days, he was a keen horse rider. Dickens would often walk for miles late at night and by doing this he would see what London was like from a different perspective to London in the daytime. The types of places Dickens would visit in London varied from the ones in his social life, like theatres, to dangerous parts of London, like the slums. It has been said that he would often go on night walks when he could not sleep. Dickens thought things through very carefully, especially the characters in his books. Many of the places he visited and socialised at, like the Ye Olde Cheshire Cheese and the George and Vulture would give him fresh ideas. The poor people that he passed by in the slums must have been a reminder of his own past and he felt pity for them. His family could have very well ended up being homeless if it were not for friends of the family who helped them out and gave them lodgings. Dickens' father's extravagant spending meant that his family often had to go without, and it eventually led to his father's debts increasing and him being sent to the Marshalsea prison.

Chapter 17
Highlighting Poverty in London

In Dickens' books, he often refers to London as a 'slum' or 'run down'. Things could have turned out very differently for Dickens, especially when he was working in the Blacking factory as a child because he spent many months alone. He would walk the streets or slums in London back and forth to work at the factory. He stayed at lodgings with a family friend and looked after himself while his mother and siblings were living with his father in the Marshalsea prison. He would carefully divide his wages into spending money for each day to buy food. He was a sensible boy who kept out of trouble and so avoided ending up like one of the characters in his book *Oliver Twist*. Dickens knew that anyone may end up being poor. He spent all his life raising awareness for the poor. His father, at one time, had a good job in the Navy pay office which paid well but he was often in debt for overspending his money and not being able to pay his bills. John Dickens would have been first sent to a lock-up-house which was the first phase of debtor's prison where the debtors would be held while they tried to raise some funds to keep them out of the prison. Being in debt was a crime in the nineteenth century and must have brought embarrassment and shame to the family as it was a very public punishment with a harsh penalty. When John Dickens was sent to the Marshalsea prison, Charles was sent to work in the factory with the ragged poor children to help pay off his father's debts. He had some private education and his family led a reasonably comfortable lifestyle so it would have felt very hard to fit in at the factory with the other children. Perhaps because of this experience it was important for Dickens to do something to help the poor. He became a social reformer in the hope that he could help the poor and unfortunate children to have a better life. He visited ragged schools and described one school that really affected him as having a 'sickening atmosphere'. He witnessed the awful conditions inside these schools, not only were the children in rags and filthy but the conditions they had to work in were equally filthy.

There was filth everywhere and an unbearable stench and disease lingered in the air. The walls, windows, floors even the desk and furniture were stained black from the filth.

Dickens' books are not all about poor children in orphanages they are also about rich and selfish people. He observed all types of people and enjoyed recreating them as characters in his books. *The Pickwick Papers* gives a good example of a cockney character, Sam Weller. From people, places and landmarks, Dickens observed everything and everyone and had a photographic memory of his experiences. We can understand so much about the world and the nineteenth century that he lived in because he wrote about them in his books. Many of the things Dickens wrote about because he had witnessed or had experienced them himself.

For example, his experience of Newgate jail is the basis for his story in *Sketches by Boz, A Visit to Newgate*. He writes with a heartfelt point of view and gives intense and upsetting details of what he witnesses in his description. He shows pity for the prisoners, especially the young offenders, some of whom were only 14 years old and in prison for 'petty crimes'. He describes the horrific cramped conditions of the prison and the ill-treatment of the inmates which not only housed men but also women and children. He writes a gripping account of the disturbing thoughts of a condemned man in Newgate. In Dickens' books, he writes about criminals, crime and punishment frequently. In those days, being sent to prison for petty crimes was not unusual. People were poor and lived in slums so often turned to crime and if they were starving would steal food. Starving, penniless young children were being sent to prison all the time for stealing food. Living conditions were shocking. Children who lived in the slums of the East End of London with their families would be all crammed into one room. The poor did not stand a chance of surviving diseases such as cholera which were often associated with poverty. Outbreaks of cholera were frequent in the nineteenth century because people drank the filthy water from the river Thames. Life was harsh for the poor ragged children and until 1829 little children were being used to crawl up inside small, cramped chimneys and many of them would get trapped inside and die from suffocation. Poor children also searched the Thames mud looking for anything they could sell. Ragged schools for ragged children seemed like a good idea but the conditions were horrendous with around 200 children cramped in a classroom and only one teacher who dished out severe punishments.

Chapter 18
Dickens the Actor

When Dickens was a child, he loved acting and the theatre and would often entertain family members. Acting was a passion that remained with him all his life and he was a good mimic. He could have been a professional actor. The story goes that Dickens had an appointment with a stage manager at a London theatre but was unable to attend because he had a bad cold. He had been practising for his audition for months and who knows, if he had not been stuck at home in bed with a bad cold, he may have been a famous actor instead of a famous writer! Going to the theatre was very important in the nineteenth century and there was plenty of entertainment in London despite the gloom and poverty. People went to the theatre, which was cheap in those days, to have a good time. Dickens loved entertainment such as comedies and pantomimes and went to the Theatre Royal in Rochester when he was a child. The Theatre Royal still exists today. He saw plays by Shakespeare such as *Macbeth* and *Richard III*. Theatres in those days would have been different from today and were noisy and filled with rowdy people.

One of the most popular types of theatre in London was called the Penny Gaff because it cost a penny to go in for a performance. There were hundreds of these small theatres in London where there would be dancing and often drunk and disorderly people would end up fighting. In Dickens' days, Punch and Judy shows were common on street corners. Today you rarely see these shows except at the seaside. They still perform and entertain people at special occasions and at public events.

Sketches by Boz gives the reader an excellent look into life in the nineteenth century with description of everyday life in Dickens' days from the streets of London to theatres, inns, pawnshops, lawcourts, prisons and the filthy, muddy River Thames. Lots of the places Dickens wrote about do not exist today so it is thanks to authors like him that we can get an understanding of our history. Dickens worked for the legal profession and as a journalist and used his real-life experiences in his books. *Sketches by Boz* were first published in 1836 when Charles Dickens was a 24-year-old news reporter in his early journalism days. When Dickens moved to Doughty Street, he was still writing under the name Boz.

Dickens had an interest in prisons mainly because his father was jailed in the Marshalsea debtor's prison. The first prison he writes about in his books is the notorious Newgate prison. Newgate prison is mentioned frequently in his books such as *Barnaby Rudge, Oliver Twist, The Old Curiosity Shop*, and *A Tale of Two Cities*. Dickens also writes about the Old Bailey being famous, as a kind of deadly Inn-yard from which,

The pale travellers set out continually in carts.

The Old Bailey was the courthouse which adjoined Newgate prison and is also used as a setting for many key trial scenes such as Fagin in *Oliver Twist*, Charles Darnay in *A Tale of Two Cities*, and Magwitch in *Great Expectations*. As a child Dickens visited his father in the Marshalsea debtor's jail and wrote about his experiences in his book, *Little Dorrit*, where Mr Dorrit is locked up in the Marshalsea. In *Oliver Twist*, Oliver is sent to work in a factory, Dickens was only a few years older when he was sent to work in Warren's Blacking factory to help pay off his father's debts while his father was in the Marshalsea prison. Dickens also visited Newgate jail as a famous author and went on a tour inside the prison visiting the cells where he spoke to the inmates which were often young children. After experiencing a hanging in Newgate, he was horrified and afterwards campaigned to abolish hanging.

Dickens had an interesting life and like most people had his fair share of his ups and downs. In the 1850s, the first public libraries were opened in England which allowed people, who couldn't afford to buy books, to go to the library to read them for free. Dickens' books have been sold all around the world and translated into hundreds of different languages. Even as early as 1846 his books are known to have been translated in Dutch.

Chapter 19
Captain Robert Falcon Scott

Dickens liked to travel and would tour faraway places like America where he would read his books to an audience. His books also travelled and sometimes to unusual places. I was surprised to learn that a copy of *David Copperfield* travelled as far as Antarctica! In 1910 Royal Navy officer and explorer Captain Robert Falcon Scott was the first British explorer to lead two expeditions to the Antarctic. His first expedition between 1901 and 1904, called the Discovery expedition, was followed by a second disastrous, Terra Nova expedition, to the South Pole between 1910 and 1913. In the tragic second expedition, he led a party of five with the aim of reaching the South Pole. Unfortunately, a planned meeting with supporting dog teams from the base camp failed to take place. It was not long before they found themselves in life threatening conditions in the sub-zero temperatures. They were stranded and had no choice but to shelter and wait for a rescue which unfortunately came too late. Tragically they died. The rest of Captain Scott's men survived by living in an ice cave for seven months. Captain Scott had taken a copy of *David Copperfield* with him on the expedition which they read to each other every night for sixty nights. When they finished reading it, geologist Raymond Priestley wrote, "We were very sorry to part with *David Copperfield*." Glossopteris tree fossils were found next to Scott's body. The fossils were heavy and it would have been exhausting to have dragged them on a sledge. They knew the importance of finding these fossil trees in Antarctica, and it must have been a very exciting discovery for them to make. The tree fossils were the first discovered fossils in Antarctica and proved that Antarctica had once been a warm continent and connected to other continents. It is amazing how many stories and historical facts you become aware of when writing a book about past events. You are discovering stories about amazing, brave people who often risked their lives so that we can progress in technology and have a better future.

Chapter 20
It Is a Small World!

It has also been interesting listening to the many stories people have been telling me about Dickens. I got really excited one day when someone told me that they knew someone who was related to Dickens. I was amazed and believed that these stories could be true at first but after a few more similar stories that went something like this, "I know someone who is a distant cousin of Charles Dickens." I soon realised that it was very unlikely to be true and people do like to sometimes believe that they have something in common with the famous author. One thing was for sure, almost everyone has heard of Dickens and my journey of having plenty to read soon led me into me writing about him. I found myself getting excited when I told people what I knew about one of the world's most famous authors. When I began reading *The Pickwick Papers*, which was Dickens first novel, I found myself enjoying reading it because it is funny and entertaining and I was surprised that Dickens had a sense of humour. I was only familiar with a couple of Dickens' books, *A Christmas Carol* about Scrooge, a tight-fisted old miser, his employee, Bob Cratchit, and Bob's sick son, Tiny Tim. I had also heard of Oliver Twist – the poor homeless riches to rags orphan who is taken under the wing of a sinister and immoral character called Fagin. These stories are not funny but sad and poignant. The story goes that the well-known phrase when Oliver is begging for more food from the master, "Please, sir, I want some more," was an idea that Dickens got from a school he attended when he wanted permission to be dismissed, he would have to ask,

"If you please, sir, may I leave off?" Dickens often wrote about real people he met in his childhood. When Dickens was 12 years old and his father was in the Marshalsea debtor's prison, he boarded with a family friend called Elizabeth Roylance at 112 College Place, Camden Town. Elizabeth was the inspiration for Mrs Pipchin in *Dombey and Son*.

Dickens was one of the most famous people of his day and liked to dress in a flamboyant style. He was known to wear brightly coloured stylish three-piece suits. It is not hard to imagine this young man writing at his desk, deep in thought, writing with his goose feather quill pen dipping it in and out of the ink pot and concentrating intensively. He would have been smiling and frowning to himself as he brought life to his characters, such as the devious Fagin in *Oliver Twist* and loveable, funny cockney, Sam Weller in *The Pickwick Papers*. Dickens had a personal connection with his fictional characters and an incredible memory of his childhood upon which many of the characters in his books were created. He had a strict schedule every day when he would write. He would get up early in the morning, around seven and have his breakfast by eight, by ten he would be settled in his study at his desk where a vase of fresh flowers would be placed. Under no circumstances was he to be disturbed when he was writing. Dickens would then work until two and stop for lunch. He was often under pressure with a deadline to finish an instalment of his latest book for his publishers but once he had created his characters, there was no stopping him. The typewriter was not available to the public until 1868 so Victorian authors wrote their books by hand with a feather quill pen that would be dipped in ink. Dickens spent his early days as a bachelor living in Furnival's Inn writing by candlelight in a cold smoky room. When Dickens moved to Doughty Street, he was living a luxury lifestyle in a big house with servants. He still worked as hard as ever at his desk every morning until lunchtime, then he would go out for a long walk. Dickens' private and personal thoughts and experiences are often expressed in his books. Dickens in his earlier days as an author described London as his magic lantern. It took me a while to really understand what Dickens meant by that but one day it dawned on me! London was the city where he was inspired. Despite the overpopulated city with poverty and crime, it was full of colourful characters of all kinds. He would observe nearly every type of person in London and would then create them as characters in his books.

Chapter 21
The Influence of Living
in London

The most important places and locations that Dickens writes about seem to be in London but he also writes about places in his childhood like Portsmouth and Kent. Dickens knew London very well and had an encyclopaedia knowledge of every hidden corner tucked away in the crowded city. Even today people can enjoy visiting places, he mentioned in his books. He never forgot the day his family moved to London when he was a child because it had a big impact on him. In his books, he often describes his characters entering London for the first time like Oliver in *Oliver Twist*. Dickens was able to write realistically as he got on with people from all backgrounds whether they were rich or poor. He understood how they lived and how the poor struggled to make ends meet in the slums of London as he visited them frequently. When Dickens walked the streets of London, he observed people and he enjoyed doing this as he would often walk for miles late at night! The story goes that one day, early in the morning in London, Dickens was seen strolling through the Docklands to the astonishment of two dock workers on their night shift. As he passed the young men, one of them looked at him in astonishment and said to his friend, "I've just seen Charles Dickens!" There was never a dull moment in London, so it gave Dickens plenty to write about. Dickens was only 21 when he wrote his first book, *A Dinner at Poplar Walk*. When he became an accomplished author, he wrote the monthly instalments of his books incredibly fast so that he could meet the deadlines and have a regular income from them. Dickens wrote most of his novels in monthly parts with each part ending on a cliff-hanger so that the reader could not wait to buy the next issue for a shilling to find out what was going to happen next.

Chapter 22
The Lost Portrait, My Visit to the Charles Dickens Museum in 2019

I wanted to include my experience of a visit to the Charles Dickens Museum because it was a memorable event and an important part of the history of Charles Dickens. The lost portrait was a portrait of Dickens that was missing for over 130 years. It was finally found, by chance, in 2019! The lost portrait was painted by a female artist called Margaret Gillies in 1843 and was exhibited at the Royal Academy in London. Shortly after it was put on display at the Academy, it went missing. I have kept a diary leading up to the discovery so you can experience my tiny part in the story. I hope you find it as exciting and interesting as I have!

February 26, 2019

I have not been this excited since my visit to the Museum of London to see an exhibition called The Cheapside Hoard: London's Lost Jewels. The exhibition consisted of an amazing collection of eye-dazzling and priceless Jacobean and Elizabethan jewels. They were discovered, by chance, in a cellar of a house being demolished in Cheapside in 1912. I have been on a very special visit to the Charles Dickens Museum at 48 Doughty Street today after hearing about 'the lost portrait'. It is a portrait of Charles Dickens that went missing and became referred to as *The Lost Portrait* of Charles Dickens. Like the Cheapside Hoard, it was discovered by chance! *The Lost Portrait* was discovered when it turned up in a general sale at an auction in South Africa thousands of miles away from the Royal Academy of Arts in London. I have gone to the museum today to hopefully find out some very exciting information on the painting. *The Lost Portrait* is a miniature portrait of Dickens painted by Margaret Gillies in 1843. Margaret Gillies and Dickens were friends and social reformers. The same week the portrait was painted Dickens was writing *A Christmas Carol* and at age 31 was already famous. It was a very important portrait of him and showed him in his prime as a young successful author. We know that Dickens sat for the portrait on July 12 at 12:00 p.m. because he wrote a letter to Margaret Gillies a few months earlier about his sitting. The letter is kept in the archives of the Charles Dickens Museum. The painting was last seen in public in 1844 when it was exhibited at the Royal Academy of Arts in London. Charles Dickens sat for the portrait aged just 31 so that it could be copied and printed in a book called *A New Spirit of the Age* (1844), edited by Richard Henry Horne. *A New Spirit of the Age* was a book of essays about the great figures of the early Victorian period. Dickens' portrait was on page one followed by portraits of Alfred Tennyson, Robert Browning, William Wordsworth, Mary Shelley and others. It was excellent timing for Dickens as he had just began writing *A Christmas Carol* and it was the perfect image to portray to the public as a young handsome and talented writer. There have been several attempts to find Charles Dickens' lost portrait which go back as far as in Margaret Gillies lifetime. Margaret Gillies showed her distress and concerns about the missing portrait in a reply to a letter in 1886 from Frederick George Kitton. Frederick George Kitton was researching Dickens and had previously written to Margaret and showed his concerns for the whereabouts of the portrait. Margaret Gillies was an elderly lady by then. He asked her if she knew what had happened to the portrait because it had not been seen since it was exhibited. When she replied to his letter, you can feel the distress as she wrote, "I have lost sight of the portrait itself." It is a remarkable portrait of Dickens and it is understandable why it had been remembered by people and noted as missing. Since it went missing in 1844, it had only ever been seen as a black and white print. The poet Elizabeth Barrett Browning after viewing the portrait shortly after it was painted said, "The dust and mud of humanity about him, notwithstanding those eagle eyes." She was very pleased and impressed with the painting.

I have a postcard of the lost portrait on my desk. The postcard is the same size as the miniature portrait which is unusual for a 'miniature' because they are usually smaller. I can see why Elizabeth Barrett Browning's described Charles Dickens' eyes as 'eagle eyes'. Dickens' eyes do seem to have a piercing stare that captures you. There would have been a huge interest to see it when it was on display at the Royal Academy. It would have been very exciting to see portraits in colour and to get an accurate likeness of the colour of someone's eyes and hair in those days. The story goes that the reason why there are not many portraits of Dickens is because he did not like having them done! He did not like having to sit down for hours while he was being painted and that does not seem to be surprising. It is well known that Dickens did not like to sit down for long as he enjoyed being active and going for long walks around London.

The portrait had been lost for more than 130 years when it was found by chance in 2017 thousands of miles away from England in South Africa! So how did the portrait get lost and how was it found thousands of miles away from home? No one is certain how it became lost and how it ended up in South Africa. Margaret Gillies' adopted daughter's brother in laws emigrated in the 1860s to Natal in South Africa, where the painting was later found. *The Lost Portrait* was purchased at an auction in the same part of South Africa where the brothers had immigrated. How the portrait was discovered in an ordinary household sales auction is an amazing story and an extraordinary discovery. The story goes that at a general sale in an auction house in South Africa in 2017, a box labelled kitchen utensils was purchased by a man who paid the equivalent of £27.00. The buyer was unaware of the valuable content inside the box at the time and was pleased with his purchase as he had his eye on the frame of the portrait rather than the portrait which did not seem to be anything special. After the box was taken home and carefully examined, the buyer decided to have a good look inside but was surprised to discover that the box not only contained the household items, he was expecting but several antiques including a brass dish, metal lobster, recorder and a mouldy portrait of a pleasant looking young man. The face on the portrait could barely be made out. It was brought to the buyer's attention that perhaps the portrait could be of someone important, so he contacted art dealers Philip Mould and Company in Pall Mall, London. He sent an email of a photo of the portrait and it was passed on to a miniatures consultant who is an expert. It was a wonderful surprise for her when she saw it. She had a feeling straight away that it was very special and was the lost portrait of Charles Dickens! Philip Mould formally identified the portrait as being genuine after research. Despite the lost portrait being layered in a yellow mould, which was obscuring part of the picture, it was clear to the experts that it was the original painting by Margaret Gillies. What an amazing joyful moment that must have been for them! You can also imagine the excitement of the buyer from the auction in South Africa when they got back to him and told him the news that it was The Lost Portrait of Charles Dickens! He would be delighted with his historical discovery and the fact that he had hit the jackpot! After weeks of restoring by expert restorers at the V&A, the mould was removed from the portrait and the portrait of Dickens was restored to its original condition. It looked as fresh as the day it was painted back in 1853 by Margaret Gillies. The portrait of Dickens is a watercolour on ivory. It is mounted in its original frame which is a gold gilded oval shaped wooden frame. The portrait is quite large for a miniature painting measuring five-and-a-half inches high. Philip Mould had the painting on display at their gallery in Pall Mall for the excited public to view from November 2018 to January 2019. It was the first time it had been on display since it was on view at the Royal Academy in 1844. It was very exciting for the public to see it for the first time as a colour painting. The latest news about the portrait is that the Charles Dickens Museum are seeking to raise £180,000 to secure *The Lost Portrait* from the owner in South Africa. They will proudly add it to their collection in the museum and it will go on display for everyone to enjoy!

As I write today, in March 2019, I am so excited to tell you that the Charles Dickens Museum has already raised around £65,000 to purchase the painting. They have been receiving generous donations from all around the world! I cannot think of a better place for the portrait to be than on the wall at 48 Doughty Street. When the portrait was painted in 1843, Dickens and his family lived at number 1 Devonshire Terrace, Marylebone, London. He lived there from 1839 to 1851 and had a 12-year lease. Sadly, it was demolished in the 1950s. 48 Doughty Street is the only house that Dickens lived in that has survived. The portrait rightfully deserves to be displayed there on the wall amongst the other family portraits and paintings of the Dickens family. I cannot wait to see the portrait myself for the first time at the museum!

Saturday July 13, 2019

I am really excited today so much so that it feels like I have got a knot in my tummy! Today I have received a letter from the Director of the Charles Dickens Museum. Her letter is dated July 8, 2019 and she is writing to let me know that the fundraising for *The Lost Portrait* is now complete! She has added, "Hurray," and I can feel her relief and excitement as if she is telling me about the news in person. Her letter goes on to explain that there is going to be a private viewing on Wednesday October 23, 2019 at the Charles Dickens Museum. I cannot believe it that I am one of the very lucky people to be invited! My invitation is on its way in the post! Did I just say that? Wow! How fortunate I am. Not only will I have the privilege of seeing *The Lost Portrait* on display in the museum for the first time, but I will also be a witness to the completion of the puzzle of Charles Dickens' Lost Portrait, that is not lost anymore! I wonder what Margaret Gillies would have said when her painting was found. I am sure she would have been absolutely delighted. It must have worried and concerned her to have known that it was missing. Sadly, Margaret Gillies passed away knowing that the portrait had been lost. *The Lost Portrait* is no longer lost. I wonder if it will still be referred to as *The Lost Portrait*? I am now going to start planning my visit for the viewing of the portrait. I am hoping to be able to talk to lots of Dickens enthusiasts like myself and ask any experts who are there questions about the portrait. This is a part of the history of Charles Dickens that I am going to be a part of! I can honestly say as I finish this paragraph that no one is more enthusiastic and excited about Charles Dickens as I am right now!

Wednesday October 2, 2019

Well, at last here it is. My invitation has arrived for the viewing of *The Lost Portrait* at the Charles Dickens Museum!

"The Charles Dickens Museum is delighted to invite you to a special private view to celebrate the arrival of *The Lost Portrait* by Margaret Gillies…" RSVP by Sunday October 13, 2019.

There is no hanging around from me, I cannot wait to go and see the portrait so by Thursday, October 3. I have already reserved my place and by the Friday had even chosen a blue formal style of dress that I think will be suitable. I will be getting back to you very soon to let you know how the evening went and my experience of seeing the portrait for the very first time! It is going to be an exciting, and an interesting evening, especially when they will have speeches from the special guest such as sponsors, and trustees. Maybe Philip Mould will be a special guest?

Wednesday October 23, 2019

I have only been back home for an hour since the special viewing for *The Lost Portrait*. It seems strange saying that. Now that I have seen the portrait as I can't really believe it! I cannot wait to tell you about it, so I am not going to wait until tomorrow until I write all this down in case I forget to mention something! I can only describe my experience this evening as being very exciting and special. I felt very privileged to have been invited and I am still buzzing with happiness. Let me start from the beginning! There was one point tonight that I thought that I was not even going to make it to the museum on time and would miss the important speeches at 7 pm when we were to arrive. The bus that I was on was on a new route, (typical to happen on one of the most exciting days of my life) so I did not travel on my usual quick route which would have literally been dropped outside the Charles Dickens Museum! Luckily, I left home early as I know that the traffic in London can be horrendous. I sat on the bus for about 15 minutes then I realised that I was going in the opposite direction to the museum! Then the bus became stuck in traffic so I quickly rang the bell to get off at the next stop and jumped off the bus and walked as fast as I could to the museum which was at least a mile away. I was sweating as I walked as fast as I could and tried not to panic as it was already approaching 6 pm! I finally arrived at the Charles Dickens Museum around 6:20 and I was early, hooray! My heart then sank and I got butterflies in my stomach as I made my way inside the museum as the reality kicked in that I was going to see the portrait at last! I was greeted at the door by two friendly members of staff who took my name and directed me into the canteen which was being used as the waiting area. It was quite empty as I'd arrived early. I looked around and said hello to a couple of people who were already there and were sitting quietly. I could tell by their faces that they were a bit nervous, but their friendly smiles told me that they were as excitement as I was!

As people continued to arrive at the museum the excitement began to build as more and more people gathered in the canteen. The room soon became full, and the chairs were soon taken as the guests sat down and waited for the evening to begin. The atmosphere was cosy and nostalgic as the lights dimmed and the large white candles in hurricane lamps were lit and placed on the tables. As the candles flickered it created the perfect atmosphere for the old Georgian house which once housed the Dickens family. The staff in the canteen offered refreshments of orange juice or wine at a pop-up bar and people began to mingle together in the now crowded room. The room echoed with people chatting and laughter. As I waited for the speeches to begin at seven, I chatted to two ladies who were sat next to me. One had travelled from Yorkshire for the event and the other told me that she was a Tour Guide for Gads Hill place in Chatham in Kent which was Charles Dickens' last home. I listened with interest as she told me so much about Charles Dickens and

Gad's Hill. As seven pm approached we were all silent as we listened to a welcome speech by the director of the Charles Dickens Museum. It was so nice to meet her in person, she was warm and friendly. She began by giving thanks and expressing her gratitude to the trustees and sponsors that had made it possible for the museum to have permanent ownership of the painting. After the speech, there was a silence for a few seconds as the room went quiet. A jolly looking man with a large portrait pendant hanging around his neck with a photo of Charles Dickens stood up and introduced himself. He looked important and began explaining that he was a trustee. I could not believe what I was hearing when he introduced himself as a descendant of Charles Dickens! Charles Dickens was his, great, great, grandfather. I can quite honestly say that I was not expecting to ever in my life meet a living relative of Charles Dickens and I can only describe my feelings at that moment as being star struck! Like most people I would have loved to have met Charles Dickens in person and see for myself what he was like. Here I was meeting a living relative, and it was the closest I would ever get to meeting Charles Dickens in person! I listened and observed him with curiosity and wondered whether he had any characteristics of Charles Dickens that would be obvious!

After the speeches were finished, I left the canteen and was so excited as I made my way up the stairs to the library where the portrait was on display. I was finally going to see *The Lost Portrait* at any minute now! When I got to the top of the stairs, I made my way towards the library and as I looked ahead, I could hear talking and could see that a small crowd of excited people had already gathered in front of the painting which was inside a large wooden library cabinet. Even from a distance it looked magnificent, perfectly restored, and as good as the day when it had been first painted by Margaret Gillies. The portrait was framed in a gilded gold mount with a red velvet frame. It was brightly illuminated by a lightbulb which was switched on in the cabinet. When it was my turn to have a look, I was speechless for a few seconds as I stared at the portrait and gave a sigh of satisfaction and approval as I caught my first glimpse of it. Charles Dickens seemed to be looking back at me and his eyes had a twinkle in them. I could not help but notice how handsome he looked and it was true about 'the eagle eyes' as they really did seem to capture me. This portrait by Margaret Gillies is truly special and unique and I am so pleased that it will remain in the museum so that the public can enjoy it again for centuries to come. A lady began speaking and I recognised her from the Philip Mould gallery. She was the person who had verified the portrait as being genuine. There were lots of questions being asked as people quickly gathered around her to find out about the discovery of the portrait. It was very exciting as I listened as she explained how she felt at the first moment that a picture of the portrait was sent to her to examine. As soon as she saw it, she knew straight away that it was genuine but it would have to be tested before it could be confirmed that it was *The Lost Portrait*. She explained that she was a miniature consultant from the Philip Mould art gallery and had first received an email about the portrait back in 2017 from the man who bought it from a local auction in South Africa. She went on to explain how she gets dozens of emails everyday asking her for her expert opinion on portraits. When she received the picture of *The Lost Portrait* must have been a day that she dreamed about as she knew instantly that it was very special. She went on to explain how excited she felt when she had received the email with the image of the portrait. Despite the damage to the portrait which made it hard to see properly, it was still obvious that it was Charles Dickens. Yellow mould stains covered most of the portrait. However, after further inspection it did not take her long to recognise both the technique and distinctive style of the painting and the frame even matched the examples by Margaret Gilles. When the portrait sold, the value and significance of the portrait was unknown to the auction house. It was collected with lots of other items at a house clearance after an elderly man passed away. The portrait was packed up in a box with the rest of the unwanted house contents and was taken to the local auction be sold in a general sale. The man who had bought the portrait of Charles Dickens at the auction had only bought the box of kitchen utensils as he was only interested in the frame of the portrait. Still unaware of the value of the portrait he decided to sell the frame for around 50 pounds which he was very pleased with. It is astonishing that the frame was later recovered and not lost for good! When the man sent a photo of the portrait to Philip Mauld and the authenticity of the portrait was confirmed to be the original by Margaret Gilles he was asked for the whereabouts of the frame. They presumed that the portrait had been purchased without one and if there was one it was very unlikely to be the original. The man probably couldn't believe that he had sold the original frame and was able to buy it back again from the antique dealer he had sold it to for the same amount of £50.00! It was amazing that the original portrait been recovered and the original frame that had been displayed in the Royal Academy in 1843, 130 years earlier! The portrait despite needing lots of cleaning, mainly to remove the yellow stains, only needed restoring on a small part of the black jacket that Dickens is wearing in the portrait. The portrait shows the young Charles Dickens at 31 years old in his prime. He looks healthy and glowing with his thick brown curly hair and confident smile. The story goes that Charles Dickens had a cold during his sitting for the portrait and his nose was red and this concerned him. He was very grateful that Margaret Gillies did not show this in the painting!

As I made my way back downstairs to the cloakroom to get ready to go home, I waited around for a few minutes because there was a queue at the coat stand. It was then that my eyes were drawn to a life size cut out of a middle-aged Charles Dickens. I could not help noticing how slim and charismatic he looked. Then I noticed two men chatting and could not believe it! I thought that I had seen a ghost as one of the men was the spitting image of the cardboard cut-out version of Charles Dickens. I could not stop staring at him and when he noticed I thought I had better say something to him otherwise he might think I was being very rude! I knew that Dickens' descendants were present at the museum because one of them gave a speech earlier in the canteen. "Are you related to Charles Dickens?" I blurted out. He looked surprised by my sudden question, but his smile was warm and friendly,

"Yes," he replied, "he's my great, great grandfather." I tried to hide my excitement as I spoke to him and pointed to the cardboard cut-out.

"You're his double," I said, trying not to sound too obvious. He walked over to the cut-out of Dickens, looked at it for a few seconds, and seemed amused.

"Has anyone ever told you that you're the spitting image of him?" I said, pointing to it and feeling foolish at the obvious answer to my question! He gave a laugh and said very modestly,

"Yes!" So here it is! I have finally met someone who really is related to, Charles Dickens and I know that it is 100% proof that they really are!

This was a wonderful end to my special evening at the Charles Dickens Museum which I will never forget. As I got ready to go home and put my coat on, I could not help but feel completely fulfilled and I was buzzing all the way home. I sat on the bus and wanted to tell everyone about my experience as it was more than I had ever imagined and dreamed of. The portrait is the latest edition to the museum but in my opinion the most precious as it was finally home after being lost for over a century. It is now in pride and place in the museum with the rest of the collection of portraits of the Dickens family and will be enjoyed and an interesting talking point for centuries to come! I plan to go back to the Charles Dickens Museum soon and have another close look at the portrait and take it all in again.

Wednesday November 6, 2019

It has been 9 months since I began writing this book, and reading, and researching Dickens. It seems like it is getting to the point now when all I am talking about, and reading about is, Dickens. If I see a picture of Dickens in a book, I get excited and I just want to tell family, friends, or anyone who will listen to me, all about him. Hopefully by the time I have finished my research I am going to know an awful lot more about him. I have visited the Charles Dickens Museum many times for research which has inspired my writing. It is amazing that the Charles Dickens Museum holds over 100,000 items including manuscripts, rare editions of books, personal items, paintings, furniture etc. They cannot all be displayed at one time, so the museum holds temporary exhibitions. The museum has enjoyable and very informative, guided tours and lots of different workshops to attend such as, Dickensian readings from well-known figures and entertaining performances. There are workshops suitable for all ages.

Chapter 23
Margaret Gillies (1803–1887)

Margaret Gillies was a Scottish artist born in London on the seventh of August 1803.

Margaret Gillies' father, William Gillies, was a Scottish merchant based in Throgmorton Street, London. Her mother, Charlotte Hester Bonnor, died when Margaret was only eight years old. After her mother died, Margaret and her sister Mary went to live with their uncle Adam Gillies, (Lord Gillies) where they were educated by him in Edinburgh.

Margaret returned to London in her twenties with Mary where she sought out to be a professional artist and trained to be a miniature painting artist. Margaret Gillies was well known for being a miniature portrait and watercolour artist. Professional female artists were most unusual in her day, so she must have been very special and talented. Margaret was taught by Scottish miniaturist Frederick Cruikshank. Since the sixteenth and seventeenth-century artists of miniature paintings were highly respected. The English were known to be masters at this type of painting and had a reputation for being one of the best. Miniature portraits were important because they would depict the person and their place in society. Without photographs or social media, you would not be able to see what someone looked like but with a portrait you could see a likeness. By the age of 24, Margaret Gillies had been commissioned to paint the English romantic poet, William Wordsworth. This was the romantic movement era when romantic poets and writers such as Lord Byron, Mary Shelley and William Wordsworth were famous.

Margaret Gillies was a friend of Charles Dickens; she had a lot in common with him as she shared his passion as a social reformer for those living in poverty. She painted a miniature portrait of Charles Dickens in 1843 when Dickens was thirty-one years old. The portrait was painted for a book entitled, *A Spirit of the Age*, 1844, edited by Richard Henry Horne. She died in Crockham Hill, Kent on July 20, 1887. She was buried in Highgate cemetery.

Her sister Mary was also very talented went on to become an author.

Chapter 24
Chronology

If you are new to learning about Charles Dickens, then it can be overwhelming trying to understand the significant events in his life. Below is a brief chronology of his life to help you understand his journey from a small child to becoming a famous author.

1812

Charles John Huffam Dickens is born on February 7 to Elizabeth and John Dickens in Landport, Portsmouth.

1815

John Dickens, who works for the Navy pay office, is posted to London.

1817

John Dickens is posted to Sheerness then Chatham in Kent.

1821

Charles Dickens starts at the William Giles' school in Chatham.

1822

The Dickens family move back to London, this time to Bayham Street, Camden Town.

1824

Dickens must leave school and start work at Warren's Blacking factory because his father, John Dickens, is arrested for debt and sent to Marshalsea prison.

1825

John Dickens is released from prison after his mother leaves him money on her death. Charles is sent to London's Wellington House Academy to continue his education.

1827

Charles Dickens starts work as a solicitor's clerk in Gray's Inn London.

1829

Charles Dickens becomes a freelance reporter at the Doctor's Commons.

1831

Charles Dickens works as a Parliamentary reporter.

1833

Charles Dickens' first book *A Dinner at Poplar Walk* is published in *The Monthly Magazine*.

1834

Charles Dickens becomes a reporter on the *Morning Chronicles*.

1836

Sketches by Boz is published. In Charles Dickens' earlier writing, he was known by his nickname Boz. *The Pickwick Papers* is published monthly between March 1836 and October 1837.

1836

Charles Dickens marries Catherine Hogarth.

1837

Oliver Twist is published monthly between January 1837 and March 1839. Charles and Catherine's first child, Charles Culliford Boz Dickens, is born on January 6.

1838

Nicholas Nickleby is published monthly between March 1838 and September 1839. Charles and Catherine's second child, Mary Dickens, is born on March 6.

1839

Charles and Catherine's third child, Catherine Elizabeth Macready Dickens, is born on October 29.

1840

The Old Curiosity Shop is published between April 1840 and February 1841.

1841

Barnaby Rudge is published weekly between February and November. Charles and Catherine's fourth child, Walter Savage Landor Dickens, is born on February 8. Charles Dickens tours Scotland.

1842

Charles Dickens tours America.

1843

Martin Chuzzlewit is published monthly between January 1843 and July 1844. A Christmas Carol is published in one volume in December.

1844

Charles and Catherine's fifth child, Francis Jeffrey Dickens, is born on January 15. The Dickens family move temporary to Italy.

1845

Charles and Catherine's sixth child, Alfred D'Orsay Tennyson Dickens, is born on October 28.

1846

Dombey and Son is published monthly between October 1846 and April 1848. The Dickens family visits Switzerland and Paris.

1847

Charles and Catherine's seventh child, Sydney Smith Haldimand Dickens, is born on April 18.

1848

Charles Dickens' sister, Fanny Burnett, dies on September 2.

1849

David Copperfield is published monthly between May 1849 and November 1850. Charles and Catherine's eighth child, Henry Fielding Dickens, is born on January 16.

1850

Charles and Catherine's Dickens' ninth child, Dora Annie Dickens, is born on August 16.

1851

Dora Annie and Dickens' father, John Dickens, die.

1852

Bleak House is published monthly between March 1852 and September 1853. Charles and Catherine's tenth child, Edward Bulwer Lytton Dickens, is born on March 13.

1853

Charles Dickens gives his first public readings of *A Christmas Carol* in Birmingham and tours Italy.

1854

Hard Times is published between April and August.

1855

Little Dorrit is published monthly between December 1855 and June 1857.

1856

Charles Dickens buys Gad's Hill place in Higham.

1857

Hans Christian Anderson visits Charles Dickens.

1858

Charles Dickens separates from Catherine Dickens.

1859

A Tale of Two Cities is published weekly between April and November.

1860

Great Expectations is published weekly between December 1860 and August 1861.

1863

Charles Dickens' mother, Elizabeth, and his son Walter, die.

1864

Our Mutual Friend is published monthly between May 1864 and November 1865.

1865

Charles Dickens is on the train involved in the Staplehurst railway crash. Although he is in shock, he luckily escapes any injuries.

1867

Charles Dickens tours America for the second time.

1868

Charles Dickens returns to England and tours.

1869

Doctors are concerned about Charles Dickens' health and advise him to discontinue his public reading.

1870

The Mystery of Edwin Drood is published in 1870 but is unfinished. Charles Dickens gives his last public reading on 15 March.

1870

Charles John Huffam Dickens dies on the 9th of June.

Chapter 25
St Mary-Le-Strand
Church London WC2

John Dickens married Elizabeth Barrow on June 13, 1809 at the church of St Mary-Le-Strand church in West London. Elizabeth Dickens came from a family of instrument makers. John Dickens' parents, William and Elizabeth Dickens, were servants. John Dickens worked for the Navy pay office as a clerk and he met Elizabeth Barrow through her brother, Thomas Barrow, when the two men were working at the Navy pay office.

St Mary-Le-Strand church was previously known in 1222 as the Church of the Innocents. The church was demolished in 1549 by Edward Seymour, the 1st Duke of Somerset, so that a palace could be built for him on its site. Somerset House was the first Renaissance palace in England. It was built between 1547 and 1550 for Lord Protector of England, Edward Seymour, 1st Duke of Somerset. St Mary-Le-Strand was rebuilt again in 1714 by James Gibbs in the design of English Baroque. Charles Dickens' parents married there in 1809. London churches are often featured as locations for christenings, weddings, and funerals in Dickens books.

Churches seemed to be an important part of Dickens life. Westminster Abbey and the bells chiming at St Paul's Cathedral, are also frequently featured in his books as being places where the characters frequently pass by or meet up. Charles Dickens often highlights the church bells in his books and the characters are drawn to the clocks which summon people to church or mark the passing of hours.

John Dickens' father, William, was a manservant along with his mother Elizabeth. He would have experienced the finest things in life working in a grand house. John's father would have told him about the type of people that were associated with the house and that they were very wealthy and of high status. William Dickens would have seen the lavish lifestyle that his master lived and got to know about the most expensive wines and food. Did these stories rub off on John Dickens? He also liked the finest things in life and was known to have good taste, he spoke well and dressed up like a 'proper gentleman'. When Charles Dickens was born, his birth was announced proudly in the newspaper, "On Friday, at Mile-end Terrace, the lady of John Dickens, Esq. a son." John Dickens seems to have imagined himself to be a man of an important status. The young John Dickens would have heard stories about the wealthy employers they worked for, their extravagant lifestyle and the entertaining of political figures and important people. John Dickens would have been aware of this other world and the finest things in life. Charles Dickens seems to have adopted his father's sense of style and enjoyed dressing fashionably in brightly coloured flamboyant clothing and velvet in his adult years as a writer. John Dickens enjoyed a lavish lifestyle which eventually got him into trouble and in serious debt which eventually caused him to be sent to prison. Mr Micawber in *David Copperfield* was sent to the debtor's prison just like Dickens' father and the character is said to be based on Charles Dickens' father, John Dickens. In 1812, John Dickens was transferred from London to Portsmouth and Charles Dickens was born on February 7 at one Mile End Terrace, Landport, now known as 393 Commercial Road. He was the second of eight children. A few months later in June the family moved again to number sixteen Hawke Street, Portsmouth close to the main gate of the dockyard. John Dickens could walk to work every day and had a steady job in the navy pay office that paid well. His income was up to £110 a year. In 1815, John Dickens is recalled back to London where they are relocated to Norfolk Street, Fitzrovia. A couple of years later, in 1817, they move to Sheerness and then to Chatham Kent where John Dickens takes up his post in the Pay Office in the Royal Dockyard of Chatham. These will be Dickens' happiest years as the family settle into number two Ordnance Terrace, Chatham between 1817 and 1821. Dickens stayed there until he was eleven years old.

Chapter 26
First Years in Portsmouth

Dickens draws on his fond memories of 1 Mile End Terrace, Portsmouth and Chatham in his book *Nicholas Nickleby*. Life in Chatham was idyllic, his father was a clerk in the navy pay office and was responsible for keeping the payment records for the wages for the seamen in the navy. Charles Dickens would have spent his days watching the huge wooden ships and boats come into harbour and the sailors who were out in the town would have been a familiar sight. John Dickens has been described as very smart in appearance, dressing like a gentleman and despite his working-class background he spoke very well. Unfortunately, his job meant that he was often transferred to different locations and as a result his young family moved around a lot. Charles Dickens' mother, Elizabeth, came from a family of musical instrument makers, and it has been said that she was a good mimic and was able to make people laugh. It seems like Charles Dickens, who was also a good mimic, must have got his funny side from his mother. The Dickens family lived in Rochester and Chatham from 1817 to 1822. Chatham has been described as the place where Charles Dickens felt secure and had good memories. Those early years spent as a child in Chatham have been described by him as his happiest. He recalled activities that were fun for a young child, playing by the docks, breathing the fresh sea air and dreaming about sailing away on the magnificent historic war ships. He also enjoyed reading adventure books such as *Robinson Crusoe, Arabian Nights*, and books by Henry Fielding. These fed his imagination and encouraged his creativity. He also enjoyed playing in the hayfield opposite his house and the orchards and hillsides nearby. It was a safe environment where Dickens as a child felt secure and could roam around for hours with his sister Fanny. Chatham was idyllic and would have been a perfect setting for a young boy's imagination. Charles and his sister Fanny were privately educated for a few years at a Dame school while they were living in Chatham. Later Dickens went on to attend the William Giles school in Chatham in 1821.

Chapter 27
Chatham Historic Dockyard

Chatham Dockyard was a Royal Navy Dockyard located on the River Medway in Kent. It was founded in the sixteenth century by King Henry VIII as a base for the Royal Navy's ships where it once housed purpose-built warships. During the reign of Charles II, the Dockyard was also the major base for the Royal Navy. The Dockyards were closed in 1984 with the decline of shipbuilding. Chatham Dockyard is now a maritime museum following its closure. Today it remains a popular tourist attraction for the public to enjoy a museum of British maritime history and there are some amazing warships to view like the Victorian H.M.S Garnet. In Dickens' childhood, Chatham was still a port and a naval town. Living close to the harbour and the Docks, Dickens would have been used to have seeing sailors and soldiers walking around the town and watching large sailing ships with their tall masts in the Dockyards. The ancient town of Rochester with its own cathedral, castle and guildhall was only a stone throws away from Chatham. Dickens would have had plenty to see and do and went on many visits to Rochester with his father where they would go together on long walks. In 1822, Charles Dickens left Chatham after his family had moved to Camden

Town in London because his father had a new post at the Navy Pay Office headquarters at Somerset House. Charles Dickens finished his term at school in Chatham and then joined his family at 16 Bayham Street, Camden Town. John Dickens left Chatham with mounting debts that had built up over the years, leading up to his arrest. Charles Dickens watched painfully as family heirlooms and furniture were sold off. John Dickens was arrested in 1824, a couple of years after leaving Chatham and was imprisoned in the Marshalsea. The Dickens family would have to split up and life will never be the same again for the 12-year-old boy. When John Dickens is taken away, Charles Dickens had to leave the family home and go and board with a friend of the family. The worst was yet to come when he must go and work in Warrens Blacking factory to pay for his lodgings and help pay off his father's debts. This is a painful time in Dickens' life that he will never forget.

Chapter 28
Camden Town Around 1824

It's a cold dark Monday morning and a little unkempt boy called Charles, age 12, who is small for his age, sets of for work at 6 am from his lodgings in Camden Town. His landlady, Mrs Roylance, is kind and has given him some cheese and bread wrapped up in muslin for his lunch. She waves to him with pity as he nods goodbye. He hurries along because he doesn't want to be late on his first day at work. He begins his long journey of around three miles, making his way to Warren's Blacking Factory to help pay off his father's debts. His mind is too occupied with worrying thoughts and emotions to notice the cold blustery wind blowing against his face and his freezing fingertips. He is nervous and shivers as he has dreaded this day for so long. He has no one to turn to and no one to comfort him, his father is in the Marshalsea prison with his family apart from his sister who is at school. He wonders what it is going to be like working in the factory and how on earth he will have the strength to work ten long hours a day for six shillings a week to help pay off his father's debts. He feels afraid as he remembers the rumours about the factory that terrify him. Warren's factory is on the Hungerford Stairs which is on the river. It's a filthy old wooden house, damp with rotten floors and infested with huge grey rats that come up from the cellars and run around the factory all day! He can't understand how it all went wrong and why his father couldn't stop himself from his compulsive spending and endless debts. He feels anger, and pity, for his father for causing this dreadful mess that he must help fix. He misses his school in Chatham but those happy memories seem like a dream now. He knows he must be brave but doesn't know how to be. He must put on the best act of his life and look tough and streetwise so he can fit in with the other boys and somehow survive this misery.

Chapter 29
More Misery

When John Dickens is taken away to the Marshalsea debtor's prison in Southwark, his wife Elizabeth and Charles' younger siblings join him, this wasn't unusual in those days. His older sister Fanny remained at the Royal Academy of Music in London to continue her education. Charles Dickens was distraught that he must leave school and work in the factory, and he may have felt that he was treated unfairly because his sister was able to continue her studies. His experience of working in the factory and his father's imprisonment in the Marshalsea had an emotional impact on him for the rest of his life. He was lonely and miserable and felt as though he didn't really fit in at the factory. He just wanted to go back to school and really missed his school friends in Chatham. Warren's Blacking factory was a tumble-down old house which made black boot polish. The conditions in the factory were filthy and because it was next to the Thames it was rat-infested. The wood on the floorboards and staircase were rotten. While Charles Dickens was working in the factory, he was taken to lodge with Elizabeth Roylance, who was a friend of the family at Little College Street Camden Town. It appears Elizabeth Roylance took good care of Charles Dickens while he was lodging with her. He later moved to new lodgings in a back attic in Lant Street in Southwark which was near the Marshalsea prison. Here he lodged with Archibald Russel and his family. Archibald Russel worked for the Insolvent Court. The location was convenient for him to visit his family in the Marshalsea prison so he could visit his family early in the morning for breakfast before he started work in the factory and have supper with them afterwards. On Sunday, he would spend the whole day at the Marshalsea prison with his sister Fanny who had the day off from her studies. Like many of the people he met in his childhood, Charles Dickens' characters are often based on real people he met but changed their names. The character Mrs Pipchin, in *Dombey and Son*, is based on Elizabeth Roylance. Bob Fagin, in *Oliver Twist*, is based on a boy that befriended Charles Dickens when he was twelve years old while working with him in the Blacking factory whose name was Bob Fagin! A few months after John Dickens' imprisonment, his mother died and bequeathed him four hundred and fifty pounds. With this money, he was able to pay off his debts and be released from prison under the Insolvent Debtors Act. After John Dickens is released from prison, his family moved back to Little College Street to stay with Elizabeth Roylance again but by the end of the year they had moved to Somers Town. The story goes that Charles Dickens' mother did not rush to take him out of the factory despite knowing about the harsh conditions and how unhappy he was there. He never understood why she behaved this way and never forgave her. In his biography written by John Forster, Dickens speaks about his experience. John Forster was his trusted friend and biographer. "I never afterwards forgot, I never can forget that my mother was warm for my being sent back." Charles Dickens' hurt and pain and loneliness can be felt from his words as he expresses his feelings about when he worked in the Blacking factory. This was a very dark time for a boy who was only twelve years old and who had previously had a normal life until then. "I had no advice, no counsel, no encouragement, no consolation, no assistance, no support of any kind from anyone that I can call to mind as I hope to go to heaven!" Shortly after Dickens left the Blacking factory, his father sent him back to school at the Wellington House Academy in Camden Town where he stayed for two years from 1825 to 1827.

Chapter 30
A Fresh Start

At age 15, Dickens left school and entered an exciting new chapter in his life as he began working as a junior clerk at Ellis and Blackmore Chambers in Holborn Court, Gray's Inn, London from May 1827 to November 1828. The story goes that his mother put in a good word in for him to a friend who worked there and then Dickens was offered the job. One of Dickens jobs was to spend the day copying out papers by hand. Dickens being a polite young man made a good impression and was very likeable. He was quick to learn and progressed in his job very quickly. He stood out from his colleagues because his clothes were flamboyant and impressive. Not only did Dickens enjoy his working life but he especially enjoyed going to the theatre. In his early days, it was at the theatre that he would spend his free time. This was a passion that stayed with him for the rest of his life and continued after he was married. His wife Catherine and their children would take part in his theatre productions. Dickens would oversee the entire performance from the lyrics, stage management and even the lighting. While Dickens worked at the law firm, he was known for his sense of humour and ability to make people laugh. He enjoyed cracking jokes and was very good at mimicking people, especially his colleagues, he could mimic the lawyers and customers, it was a trait that he inherited from his mother. It helped him create the hundreds of different types of characters in his books. His books show good examples of how adept he was at portraying characters from different backgrounds with different accents. When he was a child, he was able to recite Shakespeare and loved singing and performing. Dickens also enjoyed acting and it has been said that he could have been a professional actor and was an early member of the Garrick Club. He enjoyed entertaining the family with his sister Fanny, who went to the Royal Academy of Music. They would sing together, and Fanny would play the piano. Dickens quickly learnt the ropes at Ellis and Blackmore and began to improve his job prospects by learning how to write shorthand. He self-taught himself and learnt how to write down exactly what someone said in quick code that could be translated into English. Shorthand was a good move to further his career as it was an essential skill when he later became a journalist. At eighteen, Dickens was working as a shorthand freelance reporter in the press gallery at the Doctors Commons in Parliament as a political journalist. Now that he was able to write in shorthand, he was able to quickly write down speeches as the politicians debated the issues of the day. He soon began sketching the accounts of what he heard. Dickens loved writing his books and going to the theatre but he had many interests including geology and the sciences.

Chapter 31
First Book Published

So how did Dickens get his first book published? At 21, he wrote his first known piece called *A Dinner at Poplar Walk*. The story goes that one evening Dickens dropped off his manuscript into the letter box of the London periodical, *Monthly Magazine*. He didn't hear back from them so was quite surprised and thrilled that when he went to buy the latest issue of the *Monthly Magazine* he saw that his piece had been published. Dickens recalled that, "…my first copy of the Magazine in which my first effusion – dropped stealthily one evening at twilight with fear and trembling into a dark letter box, in a dark office, up a dark court in Fleet Street – appeared in all the glory of print; on which memorable occasion – how well I recollect it! I walked down to Westminster Hall and turned into it for half-an-hour because my eyes were so dimmed with joy and pride that they could not bear the street and were not fit to be seen there." It was the beginning of a life-long career of writing successful books and led him to become one of the most famous authors of his century. In 1834, Dickens rented a room at Furnival's Inn where he stayed for three years. In 1835, Dickens' career was progressing quickly, and he now worked for the *Morning*

Chronicle as a reporter. Dickens was now a parliamentary sketch writer and a reporter on election campaigns. Dickens would have been travelling up and down the country writing about things as they happened. Without any social media, telephones, or communication it would have had to been done in person, and it would have been hard work. He had soon visited many parts of the country including the North of England where he would have seen the industry and built up a knowledge of social indifferences. It wasn't long before Dickens was writing other kinds of articles such as commentaries on topical subjects. *Sketches by Boz* is a collection of short pieces Dickens published in popular newspapers between 1833 and 1836. They were re-issued in their current name in February and August 1836. In 1835, Dickens worked for George Hogarth where he contributed towards *Sketches of London* which were articles about scenes on London streets. In 1839, the *Sketches* were later reprinted into one book called *Sketches by Boz* when Dickens was approached by the publisher John Macrone. The illustrations were by the famous illustrator for books, and caricaturist, George Cruikshank. Dickens was not known by his real name but was known as Boz, his nickname, in his early writing. George Hogarth later became his father-in-law when he married his daughter Catherine in 1836. George Hogarth was the editor of the evening edition of the *Morning Chronicle*. Dickens was still living at Furnival's Inn, Holborn when he wrote them. The *Sketches* brought awareness of Londoners and the life of the middle and lower classes to the readers. Dickens would visit all kinds of places in London like public houses and would observe conversations. *Sketches by Boz* are real life observations of places in London Dickens knew, such as life on the streets, trades, law Courts, inns, pawn brokers, Hackney coaches, prisons, river Thames etc. By reading *Sketches by Boz*, you get an amazing knowledge of London in the 1900s and a good understanding of poverty in London at that time. The success of *Sketches* led to the publication of *The Pickwick Papers*. Dickens had an amazing talent of being able to give a detailed virtual tour of London and highlighted social differences especially amongst the poor and the difficulties that they encountered. It was a huge advantage and steppingstone for his success having George Cruikshank's name and illustrations in his *Sketches*. It has been said that Dickens changed the way that stories were written when he went on to write a monthly tale about a group of friends in *The Pickwick Papers. The Pickwick Papers* was Dickens' first novel and was published in 1837 after the success of *Sketches by Boz*. Dickens was approached by the publishers Chapman and Hall who asked him to write a comical story to sporting scene pictures they were producing. *The Pickwick Papers* which, which was previously known as *The Posthumous Papers of the Pickwick Club*, appeared in monthly instalments with Dickens still known under the name of Boz. The illustrations were by the very talented and well-known illustrator Robert Seymour. Shortly after Seymour's tragic death Robert William Buss went on to illustrate for *Sketches by Boz* and then Hablot Knight Browne (aka Phiz). Each month for a shilling people could buy the next chapter until the story built into a full-length novel. This was the beginning of his main method of writing with each chapter unfolding the next events. This type of storytelling is familiar today and is like a series such as a soap opera that develops day by day or week by week. *The Pickwick Papers* was a comical story of cockney sporting scenes set in the countryside with many different characters whose fortunes rise and fall alongside each other. In 1837, the instalments were eventually published as a book. The main character in the novel is Samuel Pickwick, the founder of the Pickwick Club.

Chapter 32
Maria Beadnell aka
Maria Winter

In 1830, Dickens at 18 years old fell head over heels in love for the first time with 17-year-old Maria Beadnell, who was the daughter of a wealthy banker in Lombard Street. Dickens will carry a torch for Maria for many years into his middle age. Maria Beadnell's father was a banker in the wealthiest district of London but the courtship ended in 1833 because Maria's father, George Beadnell, did not approve of Dickens. Dickens was not an established author and didn't make a good impression on Maria's parents. They ended their relationship by sending Maria away to France. Maria later married Henry Winter in 1845 and Dickens married Catherine Hogarth in 1836. For years, Dickens never got over Maria and their brief romance. However, in 1855 she wrote him a letter asking him to meet up with her and his feelings quickly changed. Dora in *David Copperfield* is based on the youthful Maria and Dickens' enthusiasm to meet up with her and his feelings and disappointment for her are reflected in his book. She was no longer the youthful Maria he remembered. After Maria wrote to Dickens, he agreed to meet her and was engulfed with romantic images of her and looked forward to seeing her again. She did warn him before they met that she wasn't the youthful young lady he remembered and was no longer the youthful Maria that he'd dreamed about when he was a young man. Surprisingly Dickens was disappointed when he met her. Dickens was able to create his characters in his books and they stayed forever youthful but in real life the reality is that people age and grow old. Maria had changed, like we all do, and was now a middle-aged woman. According to Dickens was looking much her age and he found her unattractive. Maria was married with a family and was known as Maria Winter. The romantic picture Dickens had in his head was from when she was around twenty years old. It was an anti-climax when he met her after exchanging letters that she had sent him expressing her fond memories of him and her desire to see him. Maria still had feelings for Dickens and had followed his successful writing career and read his books. She had watched him as he turned into a global star and felt proud to have known him. Maria had warned Dickens in advance that she had aged and was toothless and it shocked him to say the least. Dickens spent much of his life in an imaginary world inside his books where real life was easy to block out and his characters were forever young.

Chapter 33
Catherine Thomson
Hogarth, the One!

Dickens' second romance and love was with his future wife, and mother of his children, Catherine Hogarth. Catherine was a catch and one that Dickens wasn't going to let go and he planned to marry her! He met her through her father, George Hogarth, his employer at the *Morning Chronicles*. George Hogarth was an Edinburgh lawyer who had changed careers to become a journalist. Dickens met George Hogarth in 1835 when he approached Dickens to write *Sketches of London* for him. Dickens spent a lot of time at the Hogarth's family home in Fulham, West London where he also enjoyed the company of George's three daughters, Catherine, the eldest at age nineteen and her younger sisters, Georgina and Mary. Dickens fell in love and became romantically involved with Catherine who he described as pretty with large blue eyes. Dickens, who enjoyed entertaining, was cheerful and funny during his visits to the Hogarth's home and got on with Catherine who found him to be good fun because he made her laugh. Dickens was welcomed by her parents who liked him very much and he also got on very well with her sisters. It wasn't long before he would join Catherine's family for dinner. Georgina went on to became Dickens' lifelong friend. After Dickens married Catherine in 1836, her seventeen-year-old sister Mary came to live with them and Dickens' younger brother, Frederick, while Dickens was still renting a room at Furnival's Inn. They all moved to the family house at 48 Doughty Street, London with baby Charley, it was Charles and Catherine's first home as a married couple. The success from his early book, *Sketches by Boz*, had enabled him to be able to pay for a lease on a decent house with lots of living space. Catherine's sister Mary lived with the newlyweds. It was not unusual for an unmarried younger sister to join her married sister's household to help run it and look after the children. Tragedy struck the young family when 17-year-old Mary sadly passed away in her bedroom in Doughty Street in 1837. The story goes that she passed away in Dickens' arms after feeling unwell following an evening out at the theatre with Catherine and Charles. Dickens, who was close to her, never got over the shock and loss of Mary's sudden death. It affected his writing and as he couldn't write for several months, he was unable to meet the deadline for the June instalment of *The Pickwick Papers*. Catherine was so distraught that she suffered a miscarriage. Mary became a character in one of Dickens' books, most notably, Little Nell in *The Old Curiosity Shop*. Georgina who joined Charles and Catherine's household after Mary's death became a lifelong friend to Dickens and a companion until he died on June 9, 1870. When Dickens' marriage to Catherine broke down and he separated from her, Catherine moved out of the marital home in Tavistock square in 1858 taking only one of their children with her. Georgina chose to stay with Dickens and continued running the household for him and looking after the family. She became a lifelong friend of Dickens and stayed in the house in Tavistock Square as the housekeeper and looked after the children. The character Agnes Wickfield in *David Copperfield* is based on Dickens' friendship with Georgina and Mary Hogarth. The book *David Copperfield* is said to be Dickens' favourite. Catherine spent the rest of her life living at Gloucester Crescent in Camden.

Chapter 34
Catherine (Kate) Dickens

How much do we know about Catherine Dickens feelings and her inner thoughts? She met Dickens in 1835 through her father George Hogarth and they married in 1836 after a whirlwind romance and a one-year engagement. Dickens wrote many letters to Catherine during their courtship and marriage. Catherine kept hold of these letters all her life. Sadly, there doesn't seem to be many letters from Catherine to Charles that have survived. With Dickens, we can investigate his personal life and see many of his emotions because of the letters he wrote but we can't do the same with Catherine. She was a very important lady and played a big part in Dickens' life, living with him as his wife for two decades before they separated. Catherine met Dickens when he had just started his career as an author and they shared his success together. When they moved into their first proper home at 48 Doughty Street as newlyweds, they had a wonderful and exciting future in front of them. There is no doubt that they enjoyed their company and were very much in love and a happily married couple for a long time.

Chapter 35
Fulham London Around 1835

There was a loud knock on the door of a smart, fashionable, house in a street in Fulham, London. Inside the house came excited screeches from several young girls who were expecting a visit from their father's new colleague. The visitor was a handsome young man in his 20s called Charles Dickens. George Hogarth had invited him over for dinner to meet his family. "Do come in, sir," the butler said, as he answered the door to let Charles in.

"Wait here," the butler said, as he quickly hurried off. A few seconds later a loud voice came bellowing out,

"Charles, my dear fellow, how are you?" George said. Catherine's heart soared with excitement as she heard Charles' nervous reply,

"How do you do, Mr Hogarth?"

"Thank you, thank you, well," George replied as they shook hands.

"Come and meet my family." Charles followed him into the parlour where his three daughters stood with eagerness as they waited to be spoken to. One of the sisters caught his eye as she was very pretty. Charles looked embarrassed and shy, and much younger than his twenty years.

"This is my eldest daughter Catherine," George said as he signalled to her to come over. Her younger sisters giggled as they watched with amusement. Catherine felt awkward and shy as she walked towards her father and Charles. She looked radiant in her rose-pink silk dress, her pearl drop earrings dangling elegantly from her ears and her golden hair arranged in rows of curls on each side of her small round face. Her blue eyes matched his as they laughed at the same time and stared at each other smiling. Catherine's heart raced with excitement; she was certain from that very first moment that she'd fallen in love with him. He was of medium height and had long thick curly brown hair. He was wearing a blue wool frock coat and his red silk cravat was tied neatly around his neck. He looked intelligent and his eyes beamed as he introduced himself. As their eyes met she could tell that the attraction was mutual. They chatted quietly for a few minutes then Mrs Hogarth entered the parlour beaming with pride when she noticed that her eldest daughter was standing next to Charles. Then the butler announced that dinner was ready to be served and they all made their way eagerly to the dining room.

Chapter 36
Catherine Thomson Hogarth

Catherine Thomson Hogarth was born on May 19, 1815 in Edinburgh, Scotland. She moved to England with her family when she was around seven years old. When she met Dickens, she was 19 years old. She came from large middle class Scottish family who settled in London. She was the eldest of ten siblings and although she was not allowed to have an education, she was intelligent and could speak French, sew, and play the piano. She was from a respected family that had good literary connections. Her father was an editor and friends with the Scottish novelist and poet Sir Walter Scott who was a regular visitor to the family home. The story goes that Dickens was a fan of Sir Walter Scott and enjoyed listening to the stories about him told by George Hogarth. Catherine could have been a character straight out of a Jane Austen book! She was the perfect catch for the right suitor! Catherine was described as pretty with large blue eyes, neat hair kept in ringlets and could hold a conversation. She was talkative, witty and funny. It's not surprising that Dickens fell head over heels in love with her. Catherine and Charles got engaged in 1835 and after a whirlwind romance married in 1836 spending their honeymoon in a cosy cottage in Chalk, Kent. Catherine was a good mother, an excellent wife and homemaker. Dickens' early letters to her, which are now in the British Library, show that they were very much in love. One of the letters he wrote her, he adoringly calls her 'Dearest mouse'. In 1851, Catherine wrote a successful book on cooking and entertaining that's still in print today called *What Shall we Have for Dinner?* written under the pseudonym of Lady Maria Clutterbuck. She wrote sophisticated menus which catered for at least eighteen people! There is no doubt that Catherine was intelligent and an enormous contributor to their marriage. In the early days, Catherine was very much a part of Dickens' theatre productions where the whole family including the children would take part. They enjoyed going to the theatre together as a couple and Catherine was good company so for a long-time family life was pleasant. Catherine had ten children and it seems that this was one of the reasons why her marriage broke down as Dickens found this to be a strain on their relationship. It was more of a strain for Catherine because her pregnancies were not easy and she was unhappy during them possibly suffering from depression. This may have caused a lack of communication between the couple and could have caused them to drift apart. Catherine separated from Dickens in 1858. I can't help but feel very sad that this was a fairy tale marriage that came to an end. There is also speculation that Dickens had fallen in love with another woman. It does seem unjust and unusual that Catherine had to leave her family and her home. In those days, if you separated from your husband, you had no rights and the children stayed with their father. Catherine moved out of the family home, Tavistock House, with only one child, her eldest, Charley and they lived in a house in Gloucester Crescent in Camden Town.

I'm sure that Catherine loved Dickens until she died in 1879, aged 64 because she kept the collection of love letters Dickens sent her. On her deathbed, she gave instructions to her daughter Kate, "Give these to the British museum that the world may know he loved me once." These letters had an important sentimental value to her and because of these letters survived we know that at one time Dickens loved Catherine very much. I have much admiration for Catherine Dickens, after she separated from Dickens, she remained dignified right up until the end and appears to have got on with her life alone. I was in the Dickens Museum once admiring a painting of Catherine and the stewardess came up to me, glanced up at it, and said with fondness, "Wasn't she beautiful?" I agreed. The paintings of Catherine capture a beautiful, intelligent, young lady. If Dickens hadn't become a global celebrity with so many people admiring him to the extent that they almost fell at his feet, maybe they would have had a long happy marriage.

Catherine is buried in Highgate cemetery with her infant daughter, Dora, who died in 1851 aged 7 months.

Chapter 37
Frances Elizabeth Dickens (Fanny, Older Sister of Charles Dickens)

Frances Dickens was the older sister of Charles Dickens and was born in 1810 in Landport, Portsmouth. Fanny, as she was known to the family was the eldest of the eight children of Elizabeth and John Dickens. Charles who was born two years later than Fanny was very close to her and had plenty of happy childhood memories with her. As children they enjoyed singing and entertaining family and friends with their double act. Fanny was very talented and showed a gift for music at a young age and in 1823, at the age of 23 became a student at the Royal Academy of Music in London. She would study singing and playing the piano. The fees were expensive and John Dickens struggled to keep up with the payments but Fanny went on to win prizes and merits. She studied with Ignaz Moscheles who was a pupil of Ludwig Van Beethoven. Fanny was considered to be the talented child of the family and Charles felt hurt and resentful when his schooling ended in 1824 following his father being sent to the Marshalsea prison for his debts. Fanny was able to continue her studies at the Royal Academy of Music but Charles had to work in Warren's Blacking factory to pay off his father's debts. In 1827, Fanny was taken on as a professional musician and paid by the Academy for around two years. She met her husband, Henry Burnett, at the Royal Academy during her studies there. Fanny influenced several of Charles' characters in his novels including, Little Fan, the younger sister of Ebenezer Scrooge in *A Christmas Carol*, and Florence Dombey, the beloved sister of Paul in *Dombey and Son*. Fanny married Henry in 1837 and they had two sons, Henry and Charles. Henry was a sick child, who inspired Dickens' character Tiny Tim in *A Christmas Carol*. In a letter from Charles Dickens in 1848 to his friend John Forster, Charles describes his visit to his sick sister Fanny who eventually died of tuberculosis. Dickens' painful loss of his sister is clear in his moving and emotional letter, "…such an affecting exhibition of strength and tenderness, in all that early decay, is quite indescribable. I need not tell you how it moved me. I cannot look round upon the dear children here without some misgiving that this sad disease will not perish out of our blood with her; but I am sure I have no selfishness in the thought, and God knows how small the world looks to one who comes out of such a sick room on a bright summer day. I don't know why I write this before going to bed. I only know that in the very pity and grief of my heart, I feel as if it were doing something."

Charles Dickens' much-loved sister, Fanny, died on September 2, 1848, she was only thirty-eight years old. Her son Henry died soon afterwards. They are buried together at Highgate Cemetery in London along with other members of the Dickens family.

Chapter 38
Camden Town, London
Nineteenth Century

Charles Dickens' family moved to sixteen Bayham Street, Camden Town in 1822 when his father had been posted to a new job in London and they had to leave Chatham. Charles stayed behind in Chatham to finish his studies at school and didn't join his family until 1824. In 1822, Camden Town would have been a new, large residential area, and a semi-rural area with green fields. It was one of the poorest areas of London. It's interesting that Charles Dickens never mentions Bayham Street in his novels but Camden town and the surrounding area do get mentioned many times in his books most notably in *Oliver Twist*. Bayham Street had an impact on Dickens' life because he was deeply unhappy when the family lived there. They moved into a small terrace house in a row of identical houses. Camden Town had been redeveloped in the eighteenth century and was a large residential area that had been built among the green fields. Another reason it was an unhappy time for Charles Dickens was because his father's debts began to spiral out of control. Dickens had to leave his school in Chatham after his final term in 1823 and come back to London because his father had been recalled to Navy Pay Office headquarters in Somerset House. Chatham was the complete opposite to London. He had freedom in Chatham to explore the Kent countryside where he could play and roam around in the fields. In 1824, when Dickens was 12 years old, his father was not able to pay off his creditors and was sent to the Marshalsea prison. Dickens had to board with Elizabeth Roylance, a family friend, in 112 College Place, Camden Town and start work in Warren's Blacking factory. In his biography by his friend John Forster, Dickens poured out his heart to Forster about his feelings of unhappiness and neglect when he was sent to work at Warren's Blacking factory. He felt that he'd been treated unfairly because his sister, Fanny, continued her piano studies at the Royal Academy of Music whereas he had to start work. Dickens' love of the streets and walking may have begun in Camden Town when he would often set off from Bayham Street and walk to his godfather's house in Newell Street, Limehouse. In *Oliver Twist*, Fagin tells one of his pickpockets, Noah Claypole, that Camden Town is an easy place to target young people on errands who are likely to be carrying sixpence in their hands. Many areas in London would have been areas where pickpockets would target people. In *Oliver Twist*, Charles Dickens focuses on Camden Town as one of the main areas. In *A Christmas Carol*, Bob Cratchit's family also lived in Camden Town. After persuading his father to allow him to move closer to the Marshalsea, Dickens moved to Lant Street in Southwark which was a short walk to the Marshalsea prison. He stayed with an agent for the Insolvent Court called Archibald Russell. His move to Lant Street meant that Dickens was able to spend breakfast in the morning and supper at night with his family at the Marshalsea. He slept in a back-attic in Lant Street and was much happier there. Dickens writes about the poverty and misery in London in his books but refers to his childhood in Kent as a place of peacefulness.

Camden Town was still a village in the early eighteenth-century on the edge of London with fields and footpaths and dark lanes without any street lighting. The development of Camden Town started in 1791. Camden Town is named after Sir Charles Pratt, first Earl Camden. Sir Charles Pratt was a wealthy lawyer, judge, and Whig politician. In 1791, he divided some of his land in North London into plots and leased it out so that it could be developed into over a thousand houses. The area is known today as Camden Town. Pratt Street in Camden town was named after Sir Charles Pratt. Transport in 1829 was mainly by a horse-drawn omnibuses that could only carry a few people at a time. In 1863, the first London underground line opened. People could now travel in gas-lit wooden carriages hauled by steam locomotives and come in and out of London easily. London went through great changes in the nineteenth century. Bayham Street was in one of the poorest areas in London and living there was not a happy time for Dickens especially after he had left the idyllic Chatham. John Dickens was the person upon whom Mr Micawber, struggling to pay his bills in *David Copperfield*, was based. Camden Town is also mentioned in *David Copperfield* when David goes to visit Tommy Traddles at his lodgings in Camden Town.

Charles Dickens' family soon moved from Bayham Street to Gower Street in Somers Town. Dickens' mother set up a school there hoping to ease their financial debts but the school was not a success. Not even one pupil enrolled there. There were many slum areas in London in areas like Whitechapel in the East End and Jacob's Island in Bermondsey which was located on the South bank of the Thames. Agar Town in St Pancras was one of the most derelict and impoverished areas of London. In 1847, slum clearance in London began to clear the slums and develop new roads and streets such as New Oxford Street. Charles Dickens' books drew attention to the poorest parts of London and aroused interest in them which helped to change them. New developments, like the railways, got rid of the slums and created public walks. In 1837, when Dickens moved into 48 Doughty Street work on Euston station, the first inter-city railway station, was being completed. On July 20, 1837, the station and railway opened to the public. Dickens lived in a time of great change and the expansion of the railway. The rapid expansion of the railway had profound effects on Victorian society and Dickens was able to reflect how he felt about it in his writing. Dickens' family home in Doughty Street was located near Euston station but he still wrote about traveling by horse and cart in his book *Nicholas Nickleby* but by the time he wrote *Dombey and Son* he mentions railway travel. It's an interesting thought that Dickens could have been one of the very first passengers to board a train at Euston station! When Dickens left London in 1860, 10 years before his death, lots of things had begun to make him prefer living outside of London. He was passenger in the Staplehurst rail crash on June 9, 1865 and lucky to not have been injured as some people lost their lives. He was traumatised by both being in the accident and helping the injured and dying afterwards. For the rest of his life, he was very nervous if he had to travel by train, so he avoided rail travel.

Chapter 39
Filthy London

London in Dickens lifetime would have been harsh for the poor with filthy slums and the air polluted with thick black smoke from the smog. Those in poverty had to rely on institutions like workhouses which didn't provide anything other than shelter. These were places of last resort for those with nothing. When Dickens was a young man, the most common way of travelling around London, apart from walking, would have been by a horse and coachman so the journey would have been uncomfortable on the bumpy, uneven, cobbled streets. Dickens, who suffered from regular bouts of colds, found the winters in London quite intolerable. There was no social security system in place in those days so rather than being given financial support, as people get today, the poor children would have to work for no wage in workhouses, in terrible conditions, in exchange for bed and board. In the nineteenth-century, the population in London expanded to around one million. One of the main reasons was because London was a magnet for work and was undergoing dramatic transformation on its way to become a modern city. This meant that it was easy to travel in and out of London as the city expanded rapidly. New factories were being built in the cities which offered increased work but fewer jobs were available in rural areas. Dickens' London was rapidly changing with new roads being developed like Oxford Street which linked other parts of London. Embankments were being built along the Thames making it safer for the public to walk. In the nineteenth century, punishment for crime was severe and thieves could be hanged just for stealing a few pennies. Characters like Fagin in *Oliver Twist* gave children food and shelter in return for street crime like picking pockets. There was no real police force before 1749 when the Bow Street runners were set up in the Covent Garden area. In 1829, Sir Robert Peel created a London police force based at Scotland Yard where the police were known as 'Bobbies' or 'Peelers' after Sir Robert Peel.

Chapter 40
Warren's Blacking Factory

When John Dickens was sent to the Marshalsea Debtors prison in Southwark in 1824, his son, Charles Dickens, was sent to work at Warren's Blacking factory at thirty Hungerford Stairs, Strand. He was paid around six shillings a week for pasting labels on pots of boot polish. The work was strenuous and in harsh conditions which left a lasting effect on Dickens who would go on to write about the social and labour conditions in factories in his novels. He wrote in his biography by his friend, John Forster, "How I could have been so easily cast away at such an age." Dickens' work mates would be a mixture of orphans and workers' sons. He felt very much out of place there and didn't fit in with the other boys. He felt humiliated and ashamed when he was working there. A few of the boys were kind to him though. He was known to be a sickly child and one day when he was working in the factory, he felt unwell and was looked after by the other boys until he recovered. Despite the company of the boys surrounding him in the workplace, he often felt lonely and only had an occasional visit from his mother. The factory had no safety and hygiene regulations and was not a purpose-built building. It was a rundown old house with rotted staircases and floors and, being next to the Thames, was infested with rats running up and down from the cellars. Dickens clearly remembered the terrible state of the factory in this detailed account,

"The blacking-warehouse was the last house on the left-hand side of the way at old Hungerford Stairs. It was a crazy, tumble-down old house, abutting of course on the river and literally overrun with rats. Its wainscoted rooms and its rotten floors and staircase and the old grey rats swarming down in the cellars, and the sound of their squeaking and scuffling coming up the stars at all times and the dirt and the decay of the place rise up visibly before me as if I were there again. The counting-house was on the first floor, looking over the coal-barges and the river. There was a recess in it, in which I was to sit and work. My work was to cover the pots of paste-blacking; first with a piece of oil-paper and then with a piece of blue paper; to tie them around with a string; and then to clip the paper close and neat all round until it looked as smart as a pot of ointment from an apothecary's shop. When a certain number of grosses of pots had attained this pitch of perfection, I was to paste on each a printed label, and then go on again with more pots. Two or three other boys were kept at similar duty down-stairs on similar wages. One of them came up, in a ragged apron and a paper cap, on the first Monday morning, to show me the trick of using the string and tying the knot. His name was Bob Fagin; and I took the liberty of using his name, long afterwards, in *Oliver Twist*."

The factory overlooked the muddy smelly Thames, so it is hardly surprising that the rats were swarming everywhere. His experience of working in the factory had a lasting effect in his life that was reflected in his books. The experience had a positive side as it gave him the drive to change society and become a social reformer campaigning against the social conditions and hard labour of the poor. Dickens got the name Fagin, in *Oliver Twist*, from a boy he became friends with when at the Blacking factory. The real Bob Fagin showed Dickens the ropes when he was new in the factory. The young Bob Fagin from the Blacking factory appeared to be polite and caring nothing like the cruel Fagin in *Oliver Twist*. Warren's Blacking factory would have been located near to where Charing Cross station stands today. Working in the factory would have been hard and long for six days a week. Dickens would work for at least ten hours having a lunch break around midday and a tea break in cold, damp conditions. For doing this job, he earned around six shillings a week. The money he earned, and worked so hard for, would have gone towards paying off his father's debts and paying his board with Elizabeth Roylance in Camden Town. The story goes that Dickens suffered more humiliation when the Blacking factory moved to Chandros Street. It was a busy street in Covent Garden. The boys worked in a room in which the window looked out onto the street. People outside would stand and watch them working. John Dickens was finally released from prison a few months after his mother passed away. When she bequeathed him £450, John Dickens was able to pay off his debts and was released from prison under the Insolvent Debtors Act. Despite Dickens' protest on how unhappy he was, he continued working at the Blacking factory for a few months after his father's release. In 1825, Dickens finally went to school at the Wellington House Academy in Camden Town where he remained until 1827. He did not consider it to be a good school. His book *David Copperfield* is based on his schooling there. The classroom was one big room cramped with around two hundred boys who would be seated on wooden benches laid out in rows. Much of the writing in class was written on a slate with chalk. Any disobedient behaviour to the teacher would be punished with a beating. Dickens first had a few years of private schooling in a Dame school and then in a school run by William Giles in Chatham, his schooling was interrupted when his father, John Dickens was imprisoned in the Marshalsea debtor's jail. Dickens left the school at fifteen when he went to work for a solicitor's firm called Ellis and Blackmore.

Chapter 41
Hardship for the Poor

Dickens wrote often about the hardship experienced by the poor and their living conditions and was a social reformer. Houses for the poor often had whole families crammed into a single room. Until 1829 small children were still being used to crawl up chimneys and clean them, they were known as Chimney sweeps. There was plenty of entertainment in London to help brighten up the miserable life like the Penny Gaff. There were hundreds of these small theatres in London which had dancing and singing! The Punch and Judy man with his puppet show was a common sight on street corners. Poor Londoners who could not read or write because education was a privilege for the wealthy enjoyed listening to the stories. In 1844, ragged schools became available for poor ragged children. They were a charitable organisation for free education however the conditions of these schools were often bad. Dickens was often troubled by the stories he'd heard about the welfare of the children in poor schools so he would also go and visit some to see for himself. He visited the Field Lane Ragged school and was appalled by the conditions. Dickens wrote about schools in his books as if they weren't much better than prisons and about schoolteachers as if they were not very good people. He would visit schools, mills and other places where he wanted to see the conditions for himself and often would speak out and express his concerns in his books. Dickens had painful memories of when he was 12 years old and had to work in a factory because of his past he could relate to the poor children and felt genuine sympathy. His childhood in Chatham in Kent was happy and idyllic, it was a completely different life to living in London. Chatham would have been a rural countryside with lots of outdoor space, fresh air and streams of fresh, clean flowing water. The population was small in Chatham but the population in London was huge, and the water was contaminated with diseases, the streets were filthy and were full of slums. When Dickens' family departed from Chatham with John Dickens deep in debt, it was not the fresh new start that they would have hoped for. Instead, they left under a dark cloud. Being in debt today does not necessarily have a stigma attached to it but in the 19th century it was a crime, and you would be sent to prison until your debts were paid off. The Dickens family left Kent with mounting debts and less than two years later, after settling in London, John Dickens was imprisoned. This had a devastating effect on all the family especially Charles who for the rest of his life remembered it clearly. Leaving school so suddenly to have to work in a factory was hard and those poignant memories never left Dickens and he wrote about his experiences in his books.

Chapter 42
The Marshalsea Prison
(1373–1842)

The Marshalsea prison was a notorious prison just South of the River Thames in Southwark. It was known for housing the poorest debtors, but it housed a variety of prisoners, including men accused of crimes at sea (smugglers and pirates) and political figures charged with sedition. In the eighteenth-century, nearly half the England's prison population were in jail because of debt. The Marshalsea prison became known around the world through the writing of Charles Dickens whose father John was sent there in 1824. Dickens' youngest siblings, Alfred, Frederick and Letitia also went to live in the Marshalsea with their mother. Charles would visit his father on Sunday with his sister Frances who was free from her studies at the Royal Academy of Music. Charles and Frances would spend one day each week with the rest of their family. Dickens never forgets his time visiting his father and later used the prison as a setting in *Little Dorrit*. He based several of his characters on his experiences most notable in *Little Dorrit* where Amy Dorrit's father, Mr Dorrit. Mr Dorrit is in the Marshalsea prison for debts so complicated no one can help get him out. The Marshalsea prison closed in 1842 and was demolished in the 1870s. All that remains of the prison today is a high brick wall which is a grim reminder of where the prison once stood. The Charles Dickens Museum in Doughty Street has an original part of a Marshalsea prison grill. Dickens often wrote about Newgate prison and other prisons in his books. Fagin in *Oliver Twist* was imprisoned and met his end in Newgate prison. In *Barnaby Rudge*, Newgate was destroyed by fire in the Gordon Riots and Lord George Gordon died in his cell. In *The Old Curiosity Shop*, Kit Nubbles was also imprisoned in Newgate. The Old Bailey is also used as a setting for many key trial scenes in his books, such as, Fagin's trial in *Oliver Twist* and Charles Darnay's trial in *A Tale of Two Cities*. If we look at some of Dickens' best-known novels like *Oliver Twist, Great Expectations, David Copperfield* and *A Christmas Carol*, we can see that they are all written about the hardship experienced by a poor boy and reflect a part of Dickens' own unhappy childhood. In *Oliver Twist*, Oliver is an honest orphan boy who is raised in an orphanage. In *Great Expectations*, Pip is a poor humble boy who meets an escaped convict who takes pity on him. In *David Copperfield*, David is a small boy whose life becomes hard when his widowed mother re-married and he is cast out of his own home and sent to earn his living in London. This story is supposed to resemble Dickens' own childhood. A few months after John Dickens was imprisoned his mother Elizabeth Dickens died and left him £450. This allowed him to be released from prison under the Insolvent Debtors Act. John Dickens paid off his creditors and he and his family left the Marshalsea and moved into the home of Elizabeth Roylance. Dickens didn't leave the Blacking factory straight after his father was released. He was deeply upset blaming his mother because she didn't come and take him home to join the rest of the family. In his biography by Forster, he expressed how he felt, "I do not write resentfully or angrily: for I know all these things have worked together to make me what I am: I but never afterwards forgot, I shall never forget, I never can forget that my mother was warm for my being sent back." Dickens eventually left the factory and was sent back school at the Wellington Academy in Camden Town where he remained until 1827. He did not consider the Wellington Academy to be a good school and thought that the headmaster was brutal. The headmaster, Mr Creakle, in *David Copperfield* is said to be based on him.

Chapter 43
Rochester Kent, Early Years

Charles Dickens' family moved to Chatham when he was five years old. Dickens' books are mainly set in London, where he lived from when he was 12 years old but they also include references to Rochester, Kent countryside and Broadstairs. One of Rochester's most famous residents is Charles Dickens. Today the author's life is celebrated every year in Rochester with the Dickensian Christmas festival where people dress up in Victorian costumes as characters from Dickens' books. Historic Rochester has been occupied by the Romans who settled there in 43 AD where they built a bridge over the River Medway. Dickens visited Rochester while a youth living in Chatham. He wrote about Rochester in several of his books including *The Pickwick Papers*, *The Uncommercial Traveller, Great Expectations* and his last unfinished novel, *The Mystery of Edwin Drood*. Rochester Cathedral features in Dickens last novel *The Mystery of Edwin Drood*. It has been said that Dickens wished to be buried in the grounds of Rochester Cathedral. It's clear how much he loved Rochester in *The Pickwick Papers* when Mr Jingle remarks, "Fine place…glorious pile – frowning walls, tottering arches – dark nooks – crumbling staircases."

Rochester, like neighbouring Chatham, had a memorable place in Dickens' life. Dickens lived, and later died, in the nearby Gad's Hill Place, Higham, Kent. As a child, Dickens would often go on long walks with his father from Chatham to Gad's Hill Place. Dickens loved the countryside at Gad's Hill, the fresh air and long walks in nearby Cobham woods. Dickens went on to own the house and spent the last years of his life living there. Dickens used the setting in many of his book. Three of Dickens' books mention Rochester Castle, *The Pickwick Papers, Great Expectations* and *The Mystery of Edwin Drood.* Dickens got an enthusiasm for walking when he was a child when he would go for long walks in the countryside setting off from Chatham to Gad's Hill Place where the magnificent Georgian mansion stood. Dickens had dreamed of living at Gad's Hill Place since he was a child. He would walk past the huge Georgian brick mansion, built for the former Mayor of Rochester, most days with his father. One day when they both stood admiring it his father told him that if he worked hard enough, he might own it one day! That's the sort of encouraging conversation I can imagine a caring parent having with their child. Dickens' heart must have filled with pride to be told that by his father. We often focus on the negative side of Dickens' relationship with his father especially when he had to leave school to go to work in Warrens blacking factory because of his father's debts. It's clear that part of his childhood was very unhappy. These stories about Gad's Hill Place show that John Dickens, despite his faults, was just an ordinary father who wanted the best for his son. They often went on these long walks together and must have had many similar conversations. John Dickens' encouragement had a lasting effect on his small son and

Charles' determination and hard work as an author paid off. When Charles was in his 40s and an established writer, he was wealthy enough to afford the mansion when it was on sale. It remained his home until his death in 1870, aged just 58. Dickens may have spent the odd moment in Gad's Hill Place reflecting on that conversation and on those words of encouragement all those years before from his father. They obviously had a huge impact on him and perhaps gave him the determination to be careful with money and save up for the house. It was the only house that he ever owned. Charles had learnt a valuable lesson from his father who was unable to control his spending. *The Mystery of Edwin Drood* was the last and unfinished novel by Charles Dickens which he wrote at his house in Gad's Hill Place before a fatal stroke on June 8, 1870.

Chapter 44
Time to Reflect on My Book

It's nearly the end of June 2019 and it's been a while since I started writing about Charles Dickens. I'm starting to gather my own thoughts and opinions now. Dickens had a special talent for writing stories and a unique style in his time. He was able to come up with ideas for new stories and characters very quickly. He often wrote to a deadline and planned the next chapter as he went along. Once he had an idea about what the next book was going to be about, he created his characters first and the story was able to fall into place quite quickly afterwards. Dickens also had a head for business and once he became an accomplished author, he was able to negotiable publishing royalties and the copyright for his books. His father was in debt most of his life and those debts were a constant burden for Charles who bailed him out many times. This was a constant worry for Charles as the painful memory of his father being sent to the Marshalsea never went away because of his constant money troubles. Dickens as an adult, with his own large family and wife, was financially responsible and still felt responsible for paying off his father's debts. This caused him distress and sometimes anger and resentment towards his father. Dickens made sure that he worked hard on his books, meeting the deadlines working every day, often into the early hours of the morning so that he could provide for his family. He didn't want his children to have to ever go through what he had been through. Dickens based several of his characters in his books on his experience of his father being imprisoned in the Marshalsea. The first volume of his biography was published in 1872 by John Forster, revealing Charles Dickens' secret past. In particular, his father's time in the Marshalsea prison and being sent as a child to work in Warren's Blacking factory. Dickens spent many hours revealing private details to John Forster for his biography. These details were unknown to the public and would have been a complete surprise to his readers.

This evening I've finished reading several biographies about Charles Dickens. I suppose I can now say that I'm beginning to understand, and get to know the picture of, the person who wrote the amazing books. How do we really know what someone is like, especially someone like Charles Dickens, who lived more than a hundred years ago? It has been said that Dickens' characters were so real to him that he suffered with their highs and lows when he created their personalities and story lines. He would develop the characters before he developed the story. He would laugh, cry, feel angry and pity at the same time as his characters when he was writing. They were a big part of his life and he would sit in his study alone but not really alone, as he would be wrapped up in his characters and spent every day with them. He would bring them alive in his books and would imagine their conversations. You cannot but admire the unusual relationships that he had with them which made them as realistic as possible. His books were his life, his income, his fortune and his fame. He wrote nearly every day for over 30 years and found time to write even when he was away from home on holiday with his family. His characters and ideas never left him from the minute he woke up to when he went to bed. Whenever he was at home or abroad, the people he saw and met every day had an impact on him and they gave him new ideas for the storyline in his next book. Dickens would walk for miles to different parts of London where he would observe everything that was going on around him. He would visit the slums of London and would sometimes turn up unexpectedly at poor schools and workhouses. He would visit prisons where he would be able to see for himself the disturbing living conditions and the treatment of prisoners. It must have been difficult and extremely painful for Dickens during those visits as he would recall his early years when his father was in the Marshalsea prison.

From a young age, Dickens was hard working and he continued to be so until he died. His life achievement of writing hundreds of stories was possible because of his love for writing and the genuine interest he had in the people he met. He loved acting and produced several of his own productions in the theatre and even helped his books to be transformed into plays. His sense of humour, compassion and determination combined with an incredible imagination made him one of the most successful and popular writers in the nineteenth century.

Chapter 45
48 Doughty Street London

In March 1837, Dickens moved out his cramped lodgings at Furnival's Inn and into his first family home at 48 Doughty Street London with his wife Catherine and their first child, Charley, Catherine's 17-year-old sister, Mary Hogarth and Dickens' younger brother, Frederick. While Dickens was living at Furnival's Inn, he began writing *Sketches by Boz*, and the first two series were published by John Macrone with illustrations by George Cruikshank. He had also courted Catherine while he was living at Furnival's Inn and their first child was born there after their marriage in 1836. He first rented a room at Furnival's Inn as a bachelor in 1834 when he was working as a political journalist reporting on parliamentary debates and travelling across Britain to cover election campaigns for the *Morning Chronicle*. In 1835, the *Morning Chronicle* launched an evening edition, under the editorship of the *Evening Chronicles* critic, George Hogarth. Dickens met Catherine when George Hogarth asked him to work for him and he would frequently visit their family home in Fulham. Dickens married Catherine Thomson Hogarth at St Luke's church in Chelsea on the second April 1836. They went to Chalk in Kent for their honeymoon and after their return went back to Furnival's Inn for a year before moving into Doughty Street. 48 Doughty Street was a grand spacious Georgian five storey house which Dickens described as a 'Frightfully first-class family mansion, involving awful responsibilities'. There were at least twelve rooms on four floors that all needed to be cleaned and maintained so a team of employees was essential to help with the daily demands which included the cook, housemaid, nursemaid, laundry maid. The move was a big stepping-stone from his previous lodgings at Furnival's Inn which was only round the corner. Furnival's Inn on High Holborn was one of the old Inns of Chancery. After 1817, it was no longer used for legal business but was rented out as lodgings with part turned into hotel accommodation. Dickens started living at Furnival's Inn in 1834 and stayed for three years. It was at Furnival's Inn that that he began to write *The Pickwick Papers* which was original known as *The Posthumous Papers of the Pickwick Club. The Pickwick Papers* was published in 1837 in a book format while Dickens was living at Doughty Street. In the book *Martin Chuzzlewit,* John Westlock lived in Furnival's Inn and Dickens writes about a romance in Furnival's Inn between John Westlock and the beautiful Ruth Pinch. It could be that he was reflecting on his own happy memories when he was courting Catherine while living in Furnival's Inn. The house in Doughty Street was a good start to married life being a spacious house with plenty of room for a family. Dickens could continue writing in his own study room, somewhere to concentrate and write in peace and quiet. Dickens' study overlooked the back garden and he would spend hours writing and creating his new characters in there. It was in Doughty Street that Dickens completed writing *The Pickwick Papers* and wrote two new works, *Oliver Twist* and *Nicholas Nickleby*. His success with the books he wrote in Doughty Street would make him famous and known internationally allowing him to become financially secure. The big house in Doughty Street was a luxury and a far cry from Dickens' lodgings in his earlier years as a bachelor in Furnival's Inn. At Furnival's Inn, he would write in a room lit by candlelight and would often shiver in the cold room. 48 Doughty Street is an excellent example of a Georgian house. Luckily it has survived today and you can go inside as it is now a museum. The museum is decorated almost exactly as it would have been when Charles and Catherine lived there. The house would have been decorated in dark wooden furniture, fashionable patterned carpets and wallpaper. The rooms would have been painted in pink and blue with lots of mirrors hanging up on the walls which would reflect the natural day light that would flood in through the big windows. There would have been ornaments and paintings and other personnel items. We must be so grateful that 48 Doughty Street still exists today as it's the only one house that Dickens lived in that still exists. Dickens lived in other homes in London, after Doughty Street, such as Devonshire House in Marylebone Road and Tavistock House in Tavistock Square. None of these houses exist today. The last house Dickens lived in with his wife Catherine was Tavistock House. They encountered a series of unfortunate events while living there. In 1851, their baby, Dora, died and Dickens' father also died. Seven years later, Charles and Catherine separated and Catherine moved out. It does make you question whether their run of misfortune contributed to their separation. In the 1920s, the area around Doughty Street began to decline. 48 Doughty Street had been split into individual lodgings and eventually got into such a disrepair that it could have been demolished. In 1837, when Dickens moved into 48 Doughty Street, he had a three-year lease at 80 pounds a year. It was then a private, quiet residential area and had gates at either end to restrict entry which were taken care of by porters. Today many of the Georgian houses built between 1790 and the 1840s in Doughty Street have been converted into offices. The area gradually started to decline and in 1923 and the Dickens Museum, the former home of Charles Dickens at 48 Doughty Street, was by then a boarding-house being threatened with demolition. It was saved from being pulled down by the Dickens Fellowship which was founded in 1902. They raised money to buy the house, repair it and placed it under the care of a Board of Trustees. The freehold was secured when it became available in 1925 the same year that it was opened to the public as the Charles Dickens Museum. The Fellowship, which has thousands of members worldwide, is now based at the Charles Dickens Museum in Doughty Street. Today there are around eight trustees which include descendants of Charles Dickens and the members are all still as dedicated as ever to keep Charles Dickens' memory alive. It's thanks to the Fellowship's members that the museum is still operating today. Dickens' former house in Doughty Street has an interesting collection of period furniture from his home in Gad's Hill Place The collection includes the portable desk he used for public readings and the desk on which he wrote books such as *Nicholas Nickleby* and *A Christmas Carol*. There is an interesting collection of manuscripts, first editions of some of his books, and personal family items such as the family bible and his wife Catherine's wedding ring. The move to Doughty Street would have been one of the most exciting days for the 25-year-old, up and coming author, and his wife Catherine. They would have moved into their new home with only a small collection of belongings which would probably include a small quantity of furniture and furnishings that they purchased over the months whilst living in Furnival's Inn. I expect they would have been talking and laughing as they unlocked the large wooden front door together and stepped into the large spacious entrance hall. Probably looking around in amazement at the large scale of their new house. The big entrance hall that leads off to the dining room would have been used for entertaining the young married couples' friends like John Forster. George Cruikshank, the famous illustrator for his early books, would also visit him and Catherine at home. The drawing room would be a place to relax, sing, dance and drink. Catherine would have played the piano and the entertainment would run late into the night. Often hosting friends with good conversation such as authors like Charles Dickens' friend, Harrison Ainsworth who wrote many historical novels. The house in Doughty Street would be busy all year round and if visitors came at the right time, they would be lucky enough to hear Dickens read from his latest book. These readings to family and friends in Doughty Street could have been the beginning of his public readings. Dickens loved entertaining and his dinner parties would have plenty of lavish food that had been prepared by the cook and housemaids' downstairs in the sweltering kitchen. Food was especially important to Dickens because he had encountered times in his childhood when food was scarce. Dickens often wrote about food in his books. He also enjoyed eating out at places such as The George and Vulture which is an important place that he wrote about in his book *The Pickwick Papers*. There were at least nine rooms in the house which included a scullery, a washhouse, and a wine cellar. Dickens spent long hours working in his study. Today Dickens' former house at 48 Doughty Street is a now a museum that has been extended to number 49, the neighbouring house next door. The busy Dickens household would have had tradesmen popping in and out, servants going on errands and friends visiting. The neighbours in this exclusive street would have been professional people like architects, writers, and artists. Dickens went for long walks every day and often at night to the slums which would have been only a short distance from Doughty Street. The Dickens Museum has been converted into two houses. The lobby has a visitor book that is signed by hundreds of visitors that visit the Dickens Museum. One day I had a quick glance at the visitor book and saw two pages that were on display showing messages left by visitors that had been viewing the house. The messages were warm with gratitude for the opportunity to visit Charles Dickens' former family house and I felt quite moved. One of the visitors came from China and it clearly proved that Charles Dickens still had fans and followers from all over the world. A message that caught my attention went something like this, "I have read all of your novels now I have seen your house." Charles Dickens was clearly still alive in people's hearts. The museum in Doughty Street is very important because they can visit it and get a sense of closeness to Dickens. The interior of the Charles Dickens Museum is impressive and has been carefully planned to have everything in the right place so that it feels like stepping into a life-sized dolls house! It has been carefully reconstructed to the original layout painted, decorated and furnished with antique furniture. There are colourful carpets on the wooden floors and stairs, fittings and ornaments with a fine attention to detail so that it looks like a time capsule from the 1800s when Charles and Catherine Dickens lived there with their children. As soon as you step into the entrance hall in the museum, it feels like stepping into a real home. It has a homely feel and you feel yourself being transported into the past. It's incredible that so many personal items which belonged to Charles Dickens has survived. It is a privilege to see his writing desk in the study where the young man wrote *Oliver Twist* and created characters such as Fagin, the Artful Dodger and Bill Sikes. Visiting Doughty Street may be the closest you will ever get to having a glimpse of the author's home life as you follow in his footsteps around his former house walking up the wooden stairs and wandering around the rooms which he once occupied. You can visit the bedroom where Catherine's 17-year-old sister, Mary Hogarth, Dickens' sister in-law, tragically died. Dickens was said to have been very shocked and devastated by her sudden death because he was very fond of her and is said to have never got over it. The story goes that she died in his arms after a sudden illness. Mary's death influenced Dickens' character Little Nell in *The Old Curiosity Shop* and Rose Maylie in *Oliver Twist*. Dickens and his family lived at 48 Doughty Street for only two years, which is not a long period but it was an important one because it is where he became famous for writing books such as *The Pickwick Papers, Oliver Twist* and *Nicholas Nickleby.*

Doughty street was a typical house for a middle-class family. Houses of this type were a status symbol indicating that you had money and were successful. In the house, there is an eight-day mahogany hall clock on the wall made by the London clock maker John Bennett. It was owned by Charles Dickens and stood in the hallway in in Gad's Hill Place in the 1860s. It is still in good working order. The ground floor leads into the drawing room. The drawing room would have been a room for Charles and Catherine to entertain their guests in the evening and after dinner. This would have been one of the happiest rooms of the house where the Dickens family and their guests would enjoy music, amateur dramatics, and dancing. As Dickens became famous many leading figures would have been entertained in this room. Good food and excellent wine would be served and enjoyed there as guests sat around the large wooden table that could seat at least ten people. When you leave the dining room, you enter the morning room, which is next door, this room would have been the family room where Charles and Catherine would spend time with the children, welcome visitors, and write letters. Charles and Catherine often wrote letters to each other when Dickens was away travelling. In their early years as a married couple, Charles often depended on her for her advice, especially with his books. Down the stairs in the basement was the kitchen. It would be managed by Catherine who was the mistress of the house. Traders would be popping in here with their supplies. Victorian kitchens, despite being warm in the winter, were often smoky from the cook's fire and stuffy with condensation on the windows as the piles of damp washed clothes would hang on wooden clothes airers to dry. Next to the kitchen would have been the scullery and washhouse where the maids washed clothes and dishes. It would have been hard labour washing the dirty laundry and time consuming. Everything would have to be washed and rinsed by hand. The house maids would also have to clean the house from top to bottom daily and get up very early in the morning to light the fires. The wine cellar in the basement would have housed a selection of the finest wines from France and Italy and kept for special guests. Upstairs, on the first floor, is the drawing room. Dickens would entertain visitors in this room. A childhood passion was the theatre where he would enjoy performing to family and friends. In this room, he would entertain guests with amateur dramatics. The most important room in the house in Doughty Street was Dickens' study. Dickens would spend hours here writing at his desk and would have a strict routine writing without distraction from breakfast to lunch. He filled this room with a large collection of books and a fresh vase of flowers would be placed on his desk every day. On the second floor was Catherine's seventeen-year-old sister, Mary Hogarth's, bedroom. It was here that the young couple experienced one of the most upsetting events of their life in this room. After a family evening at the theatre, Dickens was present in the room when Mary Hogarth suddenly felt unwell and died. Catherine and the whole family were devastated. The master bedroom is where Charles and Catherine slept. Catherine gave birth to Mary and Katey whilst living in Doughty Street. By 1852, she would have given birth to ten children. A smaller room nearby is where Dickens had his dressing room where he would wash, shave, and get dressed. Upstairs to the top of the house is the attic. The attic would have been the nursery and the servants living and sleeping quarters. Catherine had a nanny to help her look after the children. Today the nursey is part of the museum and has been focussed on Dickens' own childhood including iron bars from prison grills in the

Marshalsea prison where Dickens' father spent time for his debts.

Chapter 46
The Life of Charles Dickens
by John Forster

It's October 2020 and I've been writing about Charles Dicken for a while now. I often refer to how unhappy he was when his father was sent to the Marshalsea prison and Dickens was sent to work in Warren's Blacking factory at only 12 years old. This has been one of the things that I think most about when I write about him. Dickens also reflects about it in his biography, *The Life of Charles Dickens*, written by his friend John Forster. Forster was Dickens' close friend and adviser and was often the first person to see Dickens' manuscripts before they were published.

I began reading this biography with excitement and looking forward to getting to know a lot more about Dickens from his own words and accounts of events. John Forster spent hours interviewing Dickens. When he wrote *The Life of Charles Dickens*, the first volume wasn't published until two years after Dickens' death in 1872. John Forster started writing Charles Dickens biography in 1848 when the author was 35 years old. He used various resources and letters to write it and thanks to the biography we have a detailed account of Charles Dickens' life. Charles Dickens shared many personal and private things with Forster because he trusted him and knew him well enough to be open about his true recollections of his childhood. When Forster started writing his biography, he had no idea about Dickens' childhood. There is no doubt how happy Dickens was up to the age of ten when he was living in Chatham. Those days have been described as idyllic and I can certainly see why. Chatham was nothing like filthy polluted London. London was an overpopulated city with poor people living in the slums. Dickens had an incredible memory of his childhood and could recall things from as young as two years old like spending time with his elder sister Fanny. He recalled memories of them as they trotted around together and played in the small front garden in their house in Portsea where he was born. Fanny was the eldest of the children born in 1810. His parents, John and Elizabeth, had eight children but two died when they were infants. He remembers when he left the house in Portsea that it was snowing; and when they moved to Norfolk Street, Fitzrovia in London in 1815. They moved from London to Chatham, Kent in 1817 where his father John Dickens took up a new post in the pay office in the Royal Dockyard at Chatham. Education seemed to be very important to John Dickens. His daughter, Fanny, attended a preparatory day-school and Dickens had a few years of private education. First at a Dame school than at a school run by Willian Giles. John Dickens was earning good money working for the navy pay office so he could afford it. It was Dickens' mother who first taught him how to read the alphabet and the basics of Latin and English. He was happy and thriving as a young boy in Chatham and learning well. He wrote in *The Uncommercial*

Traveller, "All my early readings and early imaginations dated from this place and I took them away so full of innocent construction and guileless belief and brought them back so worn and torn, so much the wiser and so much the worse!" Dickens loved reading when he was a child in Chatham. His father had a small collection of books that he would enjoy reading books such as *Robinson Crusoe*, *The Vicar of Wakefield*, *Arabian Nights* and *Tom Jones*. Dickens enjoyed his father's company when he was a boy, and they went on long walks together and would often walk to Rochester. On their way, they would pass a house in Gad's Hill. It was a big grand house and Dickens would often stop outside with his father where they would both admire it. One day when they when they had stopped outside the house to admire it, Dickens father told him, "If he worked very hard, he might one day live there." Dickens never forgot his father's words and in his adult life after the success of his books he made enough money to buy the house that he had dreamed of, where he lived until his death.

Chapter 47
Charles Dickens, Lonely Journey to London from Chatham Around 1823

I waited at the station in the pouring rain, drenched to the bone, waiting for the coachman who was in no hurry to let me board the stagecoach. The horses, who seemed to be irritable and tired stamping their hooves on the ground and flicking their tails aggressively were finally unleased and replaced with fresh horses for the next journey which was going to London. The coachman signalled to me to board as he took control of the reins of the horses who were now beginning to get impatient. I heard the sharp crack of the whip and off we went with a sudden jerk. I held on tightly to my seat as the coach swayed from side to side and I was already feeling nauseous. I looked around the coach and felt alone, it was empty and I could smell mould and damp straw. I spent the whole journey on my own, not one single person joined me so there were no distractions from my miserable thoughts. I stared out of the window and felt heartbroken as the coach made its slow, uncomfortable journey to London. As the view of the green pastures slowly disappeared, I felt choked with

anguish as I guessed that this would be the last time I'd
probably see Chatham.

Dickens was only ten years old when his father was recalled from Chatham to Somerset House in London. The move affected him badly as he was left alone without his family to finish his final term at school. He travelled to London in a stagecoach all by himself as his family had already moved. He recalled his journey as being miserable as he passed by the places that he loved and adored like Chatham Dockyard, the fields and woods, and Rochester Cathedral. His heart was broken as he recollected the stagecoach journey to London as he sat alone with the smell of damp straw. He wrote about this in *The Uncommercial Traveller*, "There was no other inside passenger and I consumed my sandwiches in solitude and dreariness and it rained hard all the way and I thought life sloppier than I expected to find it." Charles Dickens spent the journey in misery, leaving behind what would turn out to be the happiest years of his life. As the dreary scenery of London got closer, he daydreamed of the fond memories of sailing on the ships with his father in Sheerness and watching the ships floating out in the Medway. When Dickens arrived in London, it wasn't long until things got much worse! The family had settled into Bayham Street in Camden Town which at the time was one of the poorest parts in London. Dickens described the house as being small and having a wretched little back garden. In Chatham, Dickens had lots of boys to play with but in Bayham there were none, and he was lonely. Next door to the house lived a washerwoman and a Bow Street officer lived nearby. He missed the world that had been full of happy days, where he played outside in the fields, playing with Fanny, reading books for hours and watching the boys play outdoor sports like cricket. He missed Fanny who was now away studying as she had gained a place at The Royal Academy of Music in 1823. Bayham street was dull and he felt isolated and alone without any friends. One of Dickens earliest memories was his father's many debts and he described that period in his life as chaotic with his father's spending getting out of control which got him into serious trouble with his creditors. Despite these problems, Dickens was very close to his father who he described as being kind-hearted and generous but he was miserable in London and missed school. At first, he had to stay at home and do errands for his father but felt cheated as his sister was studying at the Royal Academy of Music. It was a real blow for Dickens when he was taken out of school in Chatham. In those days, it was an unusual to prioritise a daughter when providing an education. Dickens' earliest memory of finding his way around London was when he visited his only two relatives who lived in London. His uncle who lived in Soho and his godfather who lived in Limehouse. Dickens remembered visiting lots of places in London and was at first taken aback by 'the immortal going-ons' at the Seven Dials in St Giles. He was fascinated by the markets in Covent Garden, which he had read about in a book. Covent Garden Market was the main wholesale market for vegetables, fruit, and flowers in central London from the seventeenth century until 1974. Dickens was familiar with the market from his arrival in London in 1822. Covent Garden is a street setting used in many of Dickens' books. David Copperfield dines in the Piazza Hotel and buys flowers for Dora in Covent Garden and Tom Pinch wanders around the market in *Martin Chuzzlewit*. In Dickens' essay, Night Walks-July 1860 in *The Uncommercial Traveller* he describes Covent Garden in detail, "Covent-garden market, when it was market morning, was wonderful company. The great waggons of cabbages, with growers' men and boys lying asleep under them, and with sharp dogs from market-garden neighbourhoods looking after the whole, were as good as a party. But one of the worst night sights I know in London is to be found in the children who prowl about this place; who sleep in the baskets, fight for the offal, dart at any object they think they can lay their thieving hands on, dive under the carts and barrows, dodge the constables and are perpetually making a blunt pattering on the pavement of the Piazza with the rain of their naked feet...there was early coffee to be got about Covent-garden Market and that was more company – warm, company too, which was better. Toast of a very substantial quality, that likewise procurable." At an early age, Dickens developed an interest in London and was finding many parts of it harrowing but also fascinating. His father's debts continued to get worse and to help improve the family's finances his mother, Elizabeth, opened a school in Gower Street but it was another disaster as not one single pupil was enrolled there. Things continued to get worse for the family and Dickens recalls not having very much for dinner as his father fell out with the butcher and the baker over his debts to them and it wasn't long before he was arrested. Dickens reveals his devasted feelings from the time when his father was taken away to the Marshalsea to Forster, "I truly believed at the time that they had broken my heart." The family possessions were soon sold or taken to the pawn shop. The books that Dickens had once read in Chatham, that he treasured so much, were the first to go to a bookseller in Hampstead. Soon followed by the family heirlooms until eventually even the tables and chairs had to be sold and house was bare.

In *David Copperfield*, David also had to sell his treasured books but to a bookseller in the City Road. The part where David visits Mr Micawber for in a debtor's prison is said to be based on a real-life account of Dickens' own life when he visited his father in the Marshalsea prison. Dickens used his painful experiences as a little boy in *David Copperfield* and combines fiction and fact but there is no doubt that Dickens has based David Copperfield on himself as a child and his father John Dickens as Mr Micawber. There are so many similarities like David's riches to rags story and the Marshalsea prison.

Chapter 48
Painful Secrets Revealed

When Dickens revealed his childhood experience of working in the Blacking factory to Forster, Forster could see how painful those memories were. Dickens told Forster in a casual conversation and until then Forster had no idea about this part of Dickens' childhood. It was at the Blacking factory that Dickens met a boy called Bob Fagin. Unlike the criminal Bob Fagin in *Oliver Twist*, the real Bob Fagin appeared to be kind to Dickens and showed him how to paste the labels on the blacking bottles. In Dickens' own words, "His name was Bob Fagin and I took the liberty of using his name, long afterwards in *Oliver Twist*." When Dickens' father was sent to prison, he first lodged at the house of a family friend in Little College Street. It was a long journey from there to visit his father so his father arranged for him to live close to the Marshalsea at Lant street. He was then able to take breakfast and supper with his family. When John Dickens was released from the Marshalsea, the family went back to living at Little College Street but Dickens had to continue working in the Blacking factory. This caused him much distress and anger towards his mother because it was her idea that he continues working at the factory. Eventually Dickens' father told him that he didn't have to work at the factory and could go back to school. Dickens never forgot his mother's decision that he continue working at the factory, "I do not write resentfully or angrily for I know all these things have worked together to make me what I am but I never afterwards forgot, I never shall forget, I never can forget, that my mother was warm for my being sent back." John Dickens kept to his word, and he took Charles out of the factory. Charles then went to school at the Wellington House Academy which was in Morning Place in Camden Town. Dickens first day at school started at seven o'clock in the morning he felt proud and relieved that he was finally going back to school and had left the dreadful factory. As he entered the school, he noticed the large notice on the board above the door which read WELLINGTON HOUSE ACADEMY. Dickens would spend the next two years there. The school was run by a harsh schoolmaster on whom Dickens modelled the headmaster, Mr Creakle, in *David Copperfield* on. At school, Dickens appeared to get on with the other boys and was known to be boisterous and to get up to mischief, like playing pranks on people. His love for the theatre was strong even in those days as he was often the leader in the school plays.

Chapter 49
School's Out for Ever

Dickens never finished his schooling at the Wellington House Academy because his parents were interested in finding employment for him again. This time it was to be a job that he would be proud about and it was the beginning of his writing career. Dickens was only fifteen years old when his parents approached an acquaintance of a friend about finding employment for him. Mr Edward Blackmore, who was an attorney in Gray's Inn, liked Dickens very much and took him on as a clerk. He described Dickens as being clever and bright. Dickens worked for Mr Blackmore as an office clerk between May 1827 and November 1828. While he was working there, he was very popular. He was considered to be funny and entertaining and able to make people laugh when he would mimic the clients, lawyers, and clerks. Dickens began to teach himself shorthand in his spare time. He left his employment working with Mr Blackmore to become a freelance reporter for a distant relative called Thomas Charlton. Thomas Charlton was a freelance reporter at the Doctors Commons and Dickens was able to share his box to report on the legal proceedings for nearly four years. In 1832, Dickens worked for the House of Commons and became a political journalist for the *Morning Chronicle*. His journalism, in the form of sketches in periodicals, formed his first collection of pieces in *Sketches by Boz* between 1833–1836. The first published writing by Dickens was *A Dinner at Poplar Walk* included in *Monthly Magazine* in December 1833. It was later republished as *Mr Minns and his Cousin*, in *Sketches by Boz*. In 1835, while Dickens was working for *Morning Chronicle*, he was approached by George Hogarth who had launched the *Evening Chronicle*. George asked him to write some original sketches that were to be called, *Street Sketches*. The sketches were of London scenes and people. Dickens went on to write regularly for the *Sketches* under the name of Boz. Boz was a family nickname that he adopted as his pen name. *Sketches by Boz* was first published in various newspapers and other periodicals between 1833 and 1836. They were collected into a book and published by John Macrone in 1839. The cover and illustrations are by George Cruikshank who was a famous caricaturist and illustrator. Dickens was living at Furnival's Inn when he began courting George Hogarth's daughter Catherine. It was a very exciting period in his life and coincided with his first years of fame as an author. On April 2, 1836, the Times newspaper published a public note announcing that, "Mr Charles Dickens had married Catherine, the eldest daughter of Mr George Hogarth." 1836 was a very exciting year and was the year when *The Pickwick Papers* was published in a serialised format between March 1836–November 1837.

Chapter 50
Broken Hearts

Dickens and Catherine returned to their lodgings at Furnival's Inn after their honeymoon in Chalk in Kent. A few months later the newlyweds moved into their new home in Bloomsbury at number 48 Doughty Street with their first son Charley, 16-year-old Mary, Catherine's youngest sister and Dickens youngest brother Frederick. It wasn't unusual in those days for the unmarried younger sister to move into the family home. She would help run the household and look after the children. While Dickens was writing *The Pickwick Papers*, which was written for amusement and to make the readers laugh, he was secretly in despair when the publication was interrupted by a tragedy. Catherine's sister Mary died in 1837 in her bedroom in 48 Doughty Street. This had a devastating effect on all the family. Dickens was not able to write for two months so the publication of the June instalment of *The Pickwick Papers* and *Oliver Twist* was delayed. Catherine and Charles were devasted and heartbroken over the shock of Mary's sudden death. It has been said that for a long time afterwards Dickens wanted to be buried next to her. To help the young couple with the grief they stayed at a farm in Hampstead for a change of scenery and to get away from the house that held so many sad memories. It was during this time in Hampstead that he was visited by his friend John Forster. John was a good friend and was there for Dickens at very crucial time in his life when he needed support and a shoulder to cry on. John was there to console him, and to listen, and the two of them become very close friends from then onwards. Dickens wrote hundreds of letters to Forster in his lifetime, some were personal and private while others were fun. He would let Forster know about his ideas for his latest book, and he also sent him his manuscripts to read for his approval. Dickens was able to open up to Forster and express his emotions to him. When he wrote *Oliver Twist*, he explained to Forster that writing the story took an extraordinary hold of him. Oliver in *Oliver Twist* who is a likeable boy having good morals and through no fault of his own ends up being poor and working in a workhouse is thought to be taken from Dickens' own experiences as a child. Even though the book is humorous, in parts, it generally focuses on the social hardness and neglect of the children of the nineteenth century. This was a topic that Dickens was very concerned about for obvious reasons.

Chapter 51
Charles Dickens' First American Tour 1842: Visit to Boston, New York City and Canada

On January 22, 1842, Dickens arrived in Boston on his first trip to the United States with his wife Catherine. By the time Dickens began visiting and touring America in 1842, he was already a big global star and admired by his American fans. Catherine and Charles were now living in Devonshire Terrace and the invitations to visit America kept pouring in. It was clear that the invitations wouldn't stop until Dickens agreed to visit. He was delighted to be invited and agreed to sail to America to see his excited and eager fans! Dickens kept an account of his travels to America in his travelogue called *American Notes for General Circulation*. It wasn't all fun though as while Dickens was in New York he gave lectures on international copyright laws and the pirating of his work in America. This did not go down very well with the press.

While travelling to America, Charles and Catherine endured weeks of sea sickness because of the horrendous weather conditions at sea. When they finally arrived in Boston, Dickens received a warm and friendly reception with crowds cheering in the street. He had barely reached dry land when nonstop invitations to make appearances started to be received. Everyone wanted to meet him so he made time for the lavish dinner parties and getting acquainted with important figures. Despite the socialising, he still found the time to visit prisons, asylums, and workhouses. He found some prisons to be especially harsh and spoke out about the conditions. Some prisons didn't have a yard for the prisoners to exercise in and the prisoners were locked up from the first time that they entered their cell until their trial, if they survived that long. Despite getting another warm reception in New York, Dickens was not always impressed and wrote about his experiences in his travelogue. After the travelogue was published, it did not go down well with some of the Americans who saw his writing as being unfairly critical. A letter Dickens wrote to Forster in 1842 describes the pressures of fame, feeling overwhelming, and the trip taking its toll on him whilst he was in America.

"I have come at last and it is time I did, to my life here, and intentions for the future. I can do nothing that I want to do, go nowhere where I want to go and see nothing that I want to see. If I turn into the street, I am followed by a multitude." The book Dickens began working on when he came back from his tour of America was *Martin Chuzzlewit*. The sales of the book were disappointing. In the book, the main character, Martin Chuzzlewit, travels to the United States. Again, the Americans considered this book to be an unfair criticism of their country. Despite his disappointments in America, Dickens loved travelling and visiting new countries. Dickens travelled to many places but his love for England never seized. He spent many months in the summer on holiday with his family in Broadstairs.

Chapter 52
Boston, Massachusetts, United States January 22, 1842

The RMS Britannia had almost finished her long voyage from Liverpool, England, as it steered into Boston Harbour in Massachusetts. There are around one hundred passengers who are sheltering inside the steamship because the weather had been horrendous with the strong winds and violent sea swaying the ship back and forth. Almost everyone was suffering from sea sickness as it had been the worst storm ever encountered. A young man called Charles, aged 29 years old, braves the deck alone but his face is almost the same colour as his green overcoat due to his recurring sea sickness. His long thick curly hair blows in his face obscuring his view as he tries to focus in front of him towards the most important port in America. Hundreds of mighty ships look gallant as they are anchored in the Boston harbour with their masts proudly displaying flags of the United States, England, and Europe. He quickly holds on tightly to the rail on the deck as he loses his balance for a second. In his other hand, he sips brandy from a tankard to calm his nerves. He begins to daydream about the wonderful adventures that lie ahead. His young wife who has been so brave is trying to find comfort from the storm as she reads a book in their cabin. She is relieved and grateful that the children have stayed at home and are safe in London being cared for by Aunt Georgina. Charles feels proud and manages a faint smile as he reassures himself how popular he has become in England and in the United States. He knows that the American people are going to shower him with attention and admiration and as soon as he steps ashore. The press will be waiting to interview him, people will be clapping and cheering, and his secretary's diary is already fully booked. He has meetings with important people including the President of the United States, John Tyler. He longs to visit the American taverns and compare them to the ones he visits in London. Then he remembers and his face suddenly frowns as he reminds himself of the important reasons behind the purpose of his trip. He feels uneasy as he gulps down the last drop of his brandy and makes his way back down to his cabin going over in his head a list of things that he will do. He will write a travelogue about slavery, visit *the prisons, institutions, and asylums. He also has a very important issue to deal with which that has been bothering him for a long, long time and keeping him awake at night. The pirating of his work in America and he is desperate to put forth the idea of an international copyright.*

Chapter 53
Devonshire Terrace

Dickens lived at number one Devonshire Terrace near Regent's Park from 1839 to 1851, the Marylebone Workhouse was nearby. The house was demolished in the 1950s. Today there is sculptured frieze on the wall where the house once stood. While he was living there, he completed *Barnaby Rudge, Martin Chuzzlewit, The Old Curiosity Shop, Dombey and Son, David Copperfield* and *A Christmas Carol.* Forster, in his biography of Dickens, describes that these years as Dickens' happiest. Despite many happy years living there and writing many books including his overnight success and best seller *A Christmas Carol*, he lost many of his family members. His sister Fanny, who he was close to, died in 1848 at only thirty-eight years old, his father, John Dickens, died in March 1851, and his daughter, Dora Annie, died as a baby in April 1851.

Charles, Catherine, and their young family moved to Tavistock House in 1851. Dickens, after his separation from Catherine in 1858 when she moved out with their eldest child, continued to live there until 1860. Dickens wrote *Bleak House, Hard Times, Little Dorrit* and *A Tale of Two cities* while there. He began writing *Little Dorrit* in 1855 as a serial publication and it was published as a book in 1857. In *Little Dorrit*, Dora's father is in prison in the Marshalsea. Dickens' father was also in Marshalsea and in 1855 Dickens went to visit the Marshalsea prison. It was no longer a prison but some of the prison rooms remained along with the outer walls. The last time he'd been inside the prison was when he was a boy visiting his father. In a letter to Forster, dated 1856, he wites, "Went to the Borough yesterday morning before going to Gad's Hill to see if I could find any ruins of the Marshalsea. Found a great part of the original building, now 'Marshalsea Place'. I found the rooms that have been in my mind's eye in the story..." While living at Tavistock House Dickens separated from his wife Catherine in 1858. Catherine moved into a property on Gloucester Crescent in Camden Town where she spent the rest of her remaining days. Tavistock House was demolished in 1901. A Blue plaque on a building nearby commemorates Charles Dickens' former home.

Chapter 54
Gad's Hill Place

Dickens bought his country home, Gad's Hill Place, in 1856 but continued living at Tavistock House until 1860. He had first seen the house in 1821 when he was a nine-year-old boy. He walked past with his father on one of their many long walks together and one morning his father stopped outside the mansion and they both stood there admiring it. His father told him, "If he worked hard enough, one day he would own it or just such a house." His childhood dream came true and once he was earning a good income from his books, he paid £1,790 to purchase the property in 1856 along with 26 acres of land. In a letter to Forster on February 13, 1856, you can tell how delighted he is with his final home, "I was better pleased with Gad's Hill Place last Saturday on going down there, even then I had prepared myself to be. The country, against every disadvantage of season, is beautiful and the house is so old-fashioned, cheerful and comfortable, that it is really pleasant to look at." Gad's Hill Place was a two-storey brick mansion with a bell turret on the roof and over the front door there was a wooden porch. Dickens continued to work in London while he was living there but it was only a matter of a few years until Gad's Hill would become his permanent country home. Those long walks with his father, as they passed by Gad's Hill Place in Higham Kent, would always remain special to him. London had been the foundation which had made him and the place where he needed inspiration to be able to write his books. Gad's Hill would be the house where Dickens would eventually spend his last days and write, *A Tale of Two Cities, Great Expectations, Our Mutual Friend* and the unfinished *The Mystery of Edwin Drood*. He would have many famous friends visit him there such as the authors Hans Christian Anderson and Wilkie Collins. Gad's Hill was only a short distance from Chatham and Dickens enjoyed many happy walks to Rochester and the Medway. Dickens separated from his wife Catherine and began focussing on something completely new which was his reading tours of Britain between 1858 and 1866 in towns in England, Scotland and Ireland. He was greeted with affection by everyone he met on the tours. In a letter to Miss Hogarth after his reading in Exeter in 1858, he wrote, "I think they were the finest audience I ever read to. I don't think I ever read, in some respects, so well, and I never beheld anything like the personal affection which they poured out upon me at the end. It was really a remarkable sight, I shall always look back at it with pleasure." Dickens often lost his voice in those early days of his readings which is hardly surprising. Dickens had always enjoyed performing. Reading to an audience of hundreds of people must have given him the spotlight that he craved for. Dickens was the perfect actor and performer and would get genuinely emotionally involved with his audience. He would laugh and cry along with them and they would cheer and clap as he read from his book and acted out his characters. He was loved and admired and looked up to by his audience. By the 1860s,

Dickens was recognised wherever he went in the country. People would stop in their tracks when they saw him and greeted him as he passed.

Chapter 55
Second Visit to America
Between 1867 and 1868

On November 19, 1867, Dickens arrived in Boston on his second American reading tour. He arrived alone not like his first trip when his wife Catherine accompanied him because in 1858, they had separated. However, he arrived as a huge celebrity and gave readings in Boston and New York. He had also planned to tour Chicago and St Louis but these were cancelled due to his health. He performed 76 readings which earned him around £19,000 between December 1867 and April 1868. In 2021, this would have been around £2.3 million. Dickens travelled between Boston and New York and gave 22 readings at the Steinway Hall in New York where he sold hundreds of tickets. His health was now beginning to decline but he stayed in America for five months which took a further toll on his health. His close friend John Forster, who was worried about his health, had advised him not to go on the tour. Despite his frail health and extreme tiredness, Dickens seemed to enjoy his second visit to America more than his first. Unlike his first tour, when he had issues about pirating, on his second visit he felt very welcome and complemented the Americans for their hospitality and on how well he had been treated during his stay. Despite his busy schedule, he visited Central Park and enjoyed the snow. Dickens left on good terms and said farewell to America with a special appearance at a banquet that the American press had organised for him.

Chapter 56
Farewell Readings

Beginning on October 6, 1868 and ending on April 22, 1869, when he collapsed in Preston, Dickens gave a series of about 100 'farewell readings' in England, Scotland and Ireland. The rushing around and long hours of reading and travelling would soon take its toll on his health and he was suffering from giddiness and fits of paralysis. Forster began to get very concerned when Dickens wrote to him and told him that he was feeling unwell. In a letter to Georgina, he told her of his struggles to read on his tours and of his feelings of sickness and sleepless nights and that it was becoming necessary to lie on a sofa all day. He was also showing signs of gout in his foot as he suffered severe foot pain which kept him awake at night. When Dickens was in Edinburgh to give a reading, he told a doctor about his dizzy spells. The doctor told him to rest for a few months because he was suffering from exhaustion due to the public readings and frequent railway journeys. On his doctor's advice, he cancelled the rest of his tours and went home to Gad's Hill Place to concentrate on his final book, *The Mystery of Edwin Drood*.

After resting and regaining his strength, he continued his farewell readings in 1870. There were 12 readings between

January 11 and March 15, 1870. He finished his final reading at St James' Hall in London. He finished with the words, "From these garish lights I vanish now for evermore, with a heartfelt, grateful, respectful and affectionate farewell." In his reading, he read from *A Christmas Carol* and the trial scene from *The Pickwick Papers*. His last public appearance was at a Royal Academy Banquet in the company of the Prince and Princess of Wales where he gave a special tribute to his friend the illustrator Daniel Maclise who had recently died on April 25, 1870. The years leading up to Dickens' death appeared to bring him pain and discomfort. His busy schedule and being overworked may have contributed to him suffering his first stroke.

John Forster saw his dear friend Charles Dickens for the last time when he dined with him in London. After Dickens' final reading, he returned to Gads Hill Place to concentrate on his book, it would be the last book he was ever going to write *The Mystery of Edwin Drood*. It was to be published by Chapman and Hall in monthly editions. He had been working on the book in a Swiss chalet which he had shipped to Gad's Hill Place when he had his second stroke. He died the next day on June 9, 1870 leaving the book uncompleted. The final plot of the book was left unresolved but Forster claims that Dickens told him that the story was about the murder of a nephew by his uncle. It was in the evening of June 8 after dinner that Dickens suffered his fatal stroke. He collapsed and struggled to stand up telling Georgina that he didn't feel well. Georgina was alarmed and could tell something was seriously wrong with Charles, she helped him to the sofa so that he could lie down, he was struggling to speak. "On the ground" were the last words that Charles Dickens ever spoke before he lost consciousness. Charles John Huffam Dickens died the next day on June 9, 1870, aged 58. His father John had died at 65. On Tuesday June 14, 1870, five days after he died, Charles Dickens was buried at Westminster Abbey and laid to rest at Poets' Corner.

Chapter 57
His Last Book, Edwin Drood

The last book Charles Dickens had been working on was *The Mystery of Edwin Drood* and it lay unfinished on his desk in his study when he died. Dickens' death was a shock to people around the world and thousands of people mourned his passing. Tributes poured in from England, America, Europe, and from around the world. Queen Victoria sent a telegram from Balmoral, "Her deepest regret at the sad news of Charles Dickens' death." Dickens' death was on the front cover of every newspaper in England and many newspapers ran obituaries. On June 14, 1870, Charles Dickens was laid to rest at Poets' Corner in Westminster Abbey. Poets' Corner in Westminster Abbey is famous for memorials for British writers, poets, scholars and intellectuals dating as far back as Chaucer who died in 1400. *The Canterbury Tales* became Chaucer's best-known work. Dickens had requested a simple burial in an inexpensive, unostentatious and strictly private manner. Although Dickens makes references to Westminster Abbey in his books *Great Expectations* and *Our Mutual Friend*, it doesn't seem to have been his wish to be buried there because one of his wishes was to be buried was in Rochester Cathedral. His request for a simple, private, memorial however was respected and the inscription on his coffin in Westminster Abbey reads:

CHARLES DICKENS
BORN 7th FEBRUARY 1812
DIED 9th JUNE 1870

John Forster and Georgina Hogarth were the executors for Charles Dickens' will and he left his personal property valued around £80,000 in their care. They were responsible for managing his personal estate, copyrights and holding the proceeds to be distributed among his children.

Georgina was to distribute Dickens' items as his will instructed her,

"I give to my dear sister-in-law, Georgina Hogarth, the sum of £8,000, free of legacy duty. I also give to the said Georgina Hogarth all my personal jewellery not herein-after mentioned, and all the familiar objects from my writing table and my room, and she will know what to do with those things. I also give to the said Georgina Hogarth all my private papers whatsoever and wheresoever and I leave her my grateful blessing, as the best and truest friend man ever had."

He bequeathed to John Forster, his loyal friend,

"I give my watch (the gold repeater presented to me at Coventry) and I give the chains and seals, and all appendages I have worn with it to my dear and trusty friend John Forster, of Palace Gate House, Kensington, in the county of Middlesex aforesaid. And I also give to the said John Forster such manuscripts of my published works as may be in my possession at the time of my decease."

Thousands of personal items that belonged to Dickens have survived and most of them are on display at the Charles Dickens Museum along with his furniture and his reading desk from his last home in Gad's Hill Place. Dickens' famous reading desk that he designed himself and was used for his American reading tours is in the Charles Dickens Museum. Dickens' desk and chair that he used in his study in Gad's Hill Place where he wrote his last unfinished book, *The Mystery of Edwin Drood*, is also on display in the Charles Dickens Museum. Dickens' home Gad's Hill Place, that he had loved and enjoyed in his middle age and dreamt of owning since he was a child, was sold as part of his estate and is now a school.

Catherine and Charles had been separated for several years by the time of his death and in his will he wrote,

"And I desire here simply to record the fact that my wife since our separation by consent has been in receipt from me of an annual income six hundred pounds."

Chapter 58
A Royal Seal of Approval

Times changed rapidly during Charles Dickens' lifetime. There were many scientific inventions such as the stethoscope, photography and the bicycle. Dickens lived for 58 years but there were four English monarchs during his lifetime. The last monarch was Queen Victoria who Dickens was said to be fond of and when they met, she commented that, "He is very agreeable with a pleasant voice and manner." As I come to an end of my book, I feel a sense of sadness as if I'm saying goodbye to someone that I didn't know but got to know quite well. Dickens took the publication industry by storm. Today publishing a book can be very competitive and it is hard work becoming an established author. In Dickens' day, without the social media that can help promote new authors and their books, it wasn't easy and there was plenty of competition. When Dickens was a child, successful authors like Jane Austen (*Pride and Prejudice* 1813) and Mary Shelley (*Frankenstein* 1818) were already successful. When Dickens was a successful writer, he was up against the Bronte sisters, Charlotte Bronte (*Jane Eyre* 1847), Emily Bronte (*Wuthering Heights* 1847), Charles Kingsley (*The Water-Babies* 1862– 1863) and Lewis Carrol (*Alice's Adventures in*

Wonderland 1865). The imaginary book started a whole new trend for children's books. Despite Dickens' lack of formal education and a childhood that encountered hardship and poverty, he had the determination to make it as a successful writer. No other nineteenth century author was like him with his multiple vocal impersonations of the characters in his books and his public reading tours. No other Victorian author had the star quality and celebrity status that he had. The morals are much the same today as in Dickens' day because if you enjoy what you do and work hard and do not give up it can lead to anyone succeeding in their dreams.

Chapter 59
Dickens, A People's Person

Dickens was a people's person. He was a social reformer and ambassador for the poor. He was quirky, approachable, likeable and had a sense of humour. He was exceptionally good at his 'day job' and had a unique style of writing fiction where he could reach out to people's hearts. He encountered many months of poverty as a child but by the time he died he was a wealthy man. His books are still as famous today as they were when he wrote them. Most people can relate to Dickens' books because they appeal to both the rich and poor and everyone can relate to his characters. The poor would queue for hours to buy the next episode of his book. He educated people who would have been otherwise unaware of how the 'other 'arf' spoke and lived. Dickens' books brought awareness of poor children and the life of hard labour that they encountered in workhouses. He opened a door in his books that welcomed everyone into his world. How could he have ever imagined that his books would never have been out of print over a century later! From a young age he enjoyed reading books, enjoyed entertaining people, and telling them stories. His love for the theatre remained with him all his life as well as his love for Shakespeare. He was a good mimic and made people laugh and the spark in his eyes was noticeable to those who met him and it remained with him until his death. As I've come to the end of my book and you finish this learning process with me, I hope you've learnt as much as I have and enjoyed reading it. Charles Dickens gave 100% to his readers, the reading tours that he gave were probably the main cause of his early death. He worked hard and never wanted to stop because he didn't want to let anyone down. When his health began to decline, he carried on with his tours, often in pain, because he wanted to give his audience the time and the loyalty that they'd given to him. What mattered more to him was the satisfaction that he gave to his readers. He campaigned and brought awareness to officials and general public of the plight of the poor, and the shocking conditions they encountered in poor schools and factories. He walked for miles around London during the day and night visiting the places he wrote about and writing about what he witnessed and experienced. He gave a detailed account of everything that mattered to him from social gatherings to social housing to law courts and prisons which so many people did not have a clue about. He went on tours to America and other European countries to promote his books and meet his fans. He travelled to America often in harsh conditions on a ship for days in the freezing cold. He would spend months away from home with non-stop travelling around the country giving public readings and personal appearances. Dickens didn't just write novels, he wrote a detailed account of life in the 1800s which has historical value. He created laughter and humour, sadness, and every emotion imagined in his books. His life was devoted to writing his books of which many have now been adapted into films or dramas for the television or the theatre.

A Christmas Carol is most probably his best-known story with many new modern adaptions.

I hope you can now take some inspiration from the 'literary genius' Charles Dickens (1812–1870). Dickens led a colourful and fulfilled life but there were plenty of voids in his adult life which caused him pain and insecurity which came from his childhood. He could express himself in his books and through his characters he could have a taste of a different past, perhaps one that he had dreamed about. His characters were escapism from his own life which at times appeared to be unsatisfactory. His life was a success story and he wrote 15 novels. He started writing like most authors unknown and struggling to make a living and was not paid for his first published work *A Dinner at Poplar Walk*. Dickens was influenced by many famous people including William Shakespeare and went on to become the most popular novelist of his time. Today he is one of the best known and most read authors. He wrote until the day he died in 1870 leaving an uncompleted book *The Mystery of Edwin Drood* on his desk at his home in Gad's Hill Place. As the curtain came down for the last time Dickens, the actor, and the author, left a huge void in people's life. No one could quite hold the attention of an audience the way that he did during his reading tours, they were the best entertainment that money could buy. His audience would be in complete silence as he played the different characters, his voice changing, sometimes scary, or sometimes sorrowful, as he became the miser Scrooge or the heartbroken Bob Cratchit. His audience would laugh, cry, and sometimes faint from the brutal scenes such as Nancy's murder in *Oliver Twist*. Oh, how I wish I could have been at one of those readings! After hearing about Dickens' death, one little girl exclaimed, "Dickens' dead? Then will Father Christmas die too?" Dickens never invented Christmas but he encouraged people to enjoy it and be merry! I think it's almost time to finish this book so I'll end with a well-known quote from *Oliver Twist*, "Please, sir, I want some more."

Bibliography

1. The London of Charles Dickens by John Greaves and A.R. Williams, published by Proof Books.

2. Dickens by Peter Ackroyd, published by Guild Publishing.

3. A Christmas Carol by Charles Dickens, English and Media Centre.

4. A Guide to Dickens London by Daniel Tyler, published by Hesperus Press Limited.

5. Dickens His Work and His World by Michael Rosen, published by Walker Books.

6. An Illustrated Map of Charles Dickens' London 1812–1870 by Kenneth William Baxendale, published by Alteridem.

7. Blogs from, The Charles Dickens Museum website.

8. The Forgotten Wife of Charles Dickens, BBC Culture, Lucinda Hawksley.

9. Charles Dickens: A Life by Claire Tomalin, published by Penguin.

10. Life of Charles Dickens by John Forster.

11. Mrs Dickens' Family Christmas BBC Two, Sue Perkins.